PENSIONS AND INSURANCE ON FAMILY BREAKDOWN

PENSIONS AND INSURANCE ON FAMILY BREAKDOWN

General editor
David Salter MA, LLM, Partner, Booth & Co, Leeds

Contributors
Roger Bamber MA, Partner, Mills & Reeve, Cambridge

Wendy Boyce LLB, Partner, Bond Pearce, Plymouth

Ian Downing LLB, Partner, Bond Pearce, Plymouth

Catherine Hallam BA, Partner, Burges Salmon, Bristol

Helen Jeavons BA, Associate, Booth & Co, Leeds

Neville Peel BA, Partner, Booth & Co, Leeds

Rebecca Rusling LLB, Solicitor, Mills & Reeve, Norwich

Lyn Yates LLB, Solicitor, Booth & Co, Leeds

The authors all practise with firms which are members of the Norton Rose M5 Group of independent legal practices.

Family Law
1992

Published by
Jordan & Sons Ltd
21 St Thomas Street
Bristol BS1 6JS

British Library Cataloguing-in-Publication Data.
A catalogue record for this book is available from the British Library.

ISBN 0 85308 168 9

Typeset by Rowland Phototypesetting Ltd, Bury St Edmunds, Suffolk
Printed at Henry Ling Limited, The Dorset Press, Dorchester

To llamas everywhere and especially the Llama of Malmesbury.

PREFACE

One of the many advantages of groupings of legal practices such as the Norton Rose M5 Group is that practitioners who might otherwise operate in comparative isolation find kindred spirits. Suddenly, the whole becomes greater than the sum total of the parts. Such has been the experience of the Family Law Group of Norton Rose M5. Early in the Group's development, it was realised that we all shared a lamentable ignorance about the subject of pensions on divorce. This we attempted to rectify by a process of self-education in our half-yearly conferences until it was suggested, with some diffidence, that the papers we had produced might be of wider interest to family lawyers. And so this book was born.

The book, therefore, is intended for the family lawyer with little or no specialist knowledge of pensions. Its primary objective is to suggest possible ways in which the 'pensions problem' on divorce, as we perceive it, may be solved on the basis of the law as it stands at present. Whilst Chapter 8 reviews various proposals for reform, we have not attempted to suggest what might be the best way forward in an area ripe for law reform.

Our thanks are due to Peter Smith, Managing Director of Norton Rose M5 Limited, for his unstinting support throughout, and to Nicola Powell, formerly of Addleshaw Sons & Latham, Manchester, for her work in the early stages of this project. To the staff at Jordans, we owe an enormous debt of gratitude for their patience and resilience. Last, but by no means least, we thank our spouses, partners and secretaries, who have enabled this book to be written.

The law is stated as at June 1992.

David Salter
Leeds
June 1992

CONTENTS

TABLE OF CASES

References to roman numerals are to the Introduction.
References to paragraph numbers are to the main text.

TABLE OF STATUTES

References to roman numerals are to the Introduction.
References to paragraph numbers are to the main text.
References to page numbers are to the precedents within the Appendix.

TABLE OF STATUTORY INSTRUMENTS

References to paragraph numbers are to the main text.
References to page numbers are to the precedents within the Appendix.

INTRODUCTION

> 'A direct and complete solution of the pension problem has . . . escaped us.'

Such was the frank confession of the Law Commission in 1969 in its first study of the problems surrounding loss of pension rights upon divorce (*Report on Financial Provision in Matrimonial Proceedings*). There the position has remained for over 20 years, leaving a former spouse – who is no longer a widow or a widower – without any entitlement under the other's pension scheme. A former wife, who may still be responsible for looking after young children or whose age is against her, is unlikely to be able to establish herself in pensionable employment, having sacrificed her own career many years ago to bring up a family. And yet the ability of the court to deal with the 'pension problem' has remained unchanged during this period. The specific reference to the problem contained in s 25 of the Matrimonial Causes Act 1973 (MCA 1973), which was unaffected by the Matrimonial and Family Proceedings Act 1984, serves only to underline the problem rather than to provide any solution. This reflects the fact that a pension is now commonly regarded as an integral part of the 'total remuneration package'. And yet as long ago as the early 1960s, pensions were talked of as part of 'the new property' (Reich (1964) 73 *Yale LJ* 733, 775).

The problem grows more acute as the number of divorcing couples of pensionable age increases. In 1990, 1 in 39 women and 1 in 44 men over the age of 65 divorced without remarrying. It is predicted that by the year 2025 the numbers will rise to 1 in 8 women and 1 in 11 men (*An Ageing Population* (Family Policy Studies Centre 1991)) The problem is further accentuated by the trend towards early retirement.

Historically, prior to the reforming legislation of 1970, matrimonial settlements were mainly concerned with income provision. Indeed, the court did not acquire the power to make lump sum orders until the Matrimonial Causes Act 1963 was passed. After that time, great energy was expended in putting together secured provision packages designed to combat the 'pension problem'. However, more recently, the clean break has become fashionable, and that has made this whole area more difficult. Recent developments, such as the Social Security Act 1990, s 8 – which effectively allows the Department of Social Security to drive a coach and horses through a clean break order where one of the parties is in receipt of income support – and the proposals contained in the Government's White Paper *Children Come First*, now enacted in the Child Support Act 1991, may reverse the trend towards the clean break.

Today, loss of pension rights on divorce is the single most neglected aspect of matrimonial finance. At worst, such losses are ignored; all too frequently the value of the loss is seriously underestimated. In reality, pension rights are usually the parties' second most valuable asset after the matrimonial home. During the course of his marriage, a husband may have had 15 per cent or more of his earnings invested in a pension fund. It is estimated that 24.4 per cent of all adults are members of contributory company pension schemes. Indeed, it is not unusual to find that pension rights constitute the parties' most valuable asset. Take the case, for example, of a headteacher who divorces in his mid-fifties with only a modest home, but who has an index-linked pension from the Department of Education and Science and many years' service behind him – the transfer value of his pension may be in the order of £150,000.

Why, then, does the 'pension problem' exist? Five reasons are suggested. First, there is no doubt that family lawyers see the complexities of pensions law and the attendant problems of non-assignability and valuation as foreign territory. However, with the spectre of professional negligence in the field of matrimonial finance looming ever larger (for example, see *Dickinson v Jones Alexander & Co* [1990] Fam Law 137), it is territory into which all must advance. Secondly, the parties themselves have more immediate concerns than pension rights amid the stress which marital breakdown imposes; both parties will be principally concerned with issues relating to the children and the future of the matrimonial home. Thirdly, a lack of resources to compensate fully for loss of pension rights is almost inevitable (see *M v M (Financial Provision)* [1987] 2 FLR 1). To state the obvious, a pension cannot simply be withdrawn as cash but this is not a reason for ignoring the problem. Fourthly, there is a general air of uncertainty about the whole problem, which may prompt arguments based upon the remoteness of the losses likely to be sustained. It may be said that the husband is many years away from retirement, even though he has already, say, 15 years' pensionable service. What is to happen in the event of loss of employment (for whatever reason), or the former wife's death or remarriage prior to the former husband's retirement? Such matters can, however, be dealt with on an actuarial valuation. Finally, in a contested hearing, the weaponry at the court's disposal is limited. Pension 'assets' are not transferable by the court. Lump sum orders or secured provision may provide a way out, and loss of pension rights may provide a defence to the imposition of a fixed term on an order for periodical payments (see *M v M* above). But, the more imaginative formulae, which are available after a negotiated settlement and which may be insurance-based, are simply not available.

On dealing with a claim for ancillary relief, one of the factors which the court must consider is the 'financial resources which the parties are likely to have in the foreseeable future' (MCA 1973, s 25(2)(a)); another factor is 'the value to each of the parties to the marriage of any benefit (for example, a pension) which, by reason of the [divorce], that party will lose a chance of acquiring' (MCA 1973, s 25(2)(h)). These exhortations do not give the court or the practitioner any practical guidance as to how to deal with the problem.

Where the problem is tackled, the approach is, in some instances, of an experimental nature. In certain divorce county courts, the proportion of the lump sum available on retirement which a wife is to receive is calculated by reference to the length of the marriage and the anticipated date of retirement. For example, a couple might get married at the age of 30 and when the husband first enters pensionable employment. The couple divorce at the age of 50 and the husband's normal retirement date is 60. In this example, the wife might get two-sixths of the husband's lump sum on retirement. However speculative this approach may seem, it is better than ignoring the problem or treating pension rights as a make-weight. But the court may only be able to adopt this type of approach where the information made available to it is limited. Indeed, it can be argued that there are dangers in adopting an approach which is too precise within a discretionary jurisdiction such as matrimonial finance. To this extent, expert evidence such as that provided by an actuary is only a means to an end (cf comments made with regard to the *Duxbury* calculation in *Gojkovic v Gojkovic* [1990] 1 FLR 140 at pp 143, 144 and 148 per Butler-Sloss and Russell LJJ).

The aim of this book is to help the family lawyer to make a serious attempt at ensuring that clients are adequately compensated for loss of pension rights on family breakdown. It has been assumed throughout, for the sake of convenience, that it is the wife who needs compensating. The reverse may be the case or, indeed, there may be mutual but differing losses.

This is not a book for the pensions lawyer and, for this reason, Chapters 1 and 2 are devoted to the basic framework of pensions. Insurance is tackled separately in Chapter 3, not only because it will often provide the right solution to the pension problem but also because it is a related area which can be used to provide maintenance protection and which is often not fully understood. The family law practitioner needs to know how life policies should be treated on family breakdown. Not all policies have surrender values and, of those which do, a surrender value may not necessarily be the correct method of valuation where bonuses lie around the corner upon maturity. In the Glossary we provide brief descriptions of many of the common technical terms relating to pensions and insurance.

After looking at how family law and pensions law interrelate in Chapter 4, Chapters 5, 6 and 7 contain our attempts to solve the 'pension problem' in practical terms. We also provide, in the Appendix, a number of precedents. It must be said that there are no easy solutions or instant answers, but it is our hope that this book may assist in dispersing the fog which surrounds this subject. This first edition is based on the law as it stands in 1992 rather than on possible future reforms.

CHAPTER 1

PENSION FRAMEWORK: STATE PENSIONS

1.1 INTRODUCTION

The main sources of law on State pension provision are the Social Security Act 1975, the Social Security Pensions Act 1975 (in both cases as amended by the Social Security Acts 1985, 1986, 1989 and 1990) and a whole army of statutory instruments regulating the State pension system's fine details. In the light of this bewildering mass of primary and secondary legislation, it is proposed in this chapter to concentrate upon those aspects of State pension provision which will most frequently confront the family law practitioner.

Beginning with a guide to present State provision, including widows' benefits, the chapter concludes with a statement of the effect of divorce upon entitlement. As will be seen, the State pension system is rigid and inflexible; the benefits provided (see Table 1) are limited and eligibility for these fairly low sums depends in the main upon the claimant having made sufficient National Insurance contributions throughout his or her working life.

In an effort to bolster the flat-rate State pension, graduated retirement benefit (GRB) was introduced in 1961 (and subsequently discontinued in 1975) and the State earnings-related pension scheme (SERPS) was introduced in 1978. Although SERPS is still operational, the benefits claimable under the scheme will be substantially reduced for those individuals retiring from the year 2000 onwards.

The State pension system does not now call for means-testing (the old earnings rule having been abolished on 1 October 1989 [1]) and is, for the most part, contributory. It is the contributory aspect of the system which is ultimately of interest to the family law practitioner when advising on the division of assets acquired by the parties to the marriage.

For a detailed exposition of the rules and regulations surrounding the State pension system, illustrated with useful examples, the practitioner is referred to Department of Social Security (DSS) publications, *A Guide to Retirement Pensions* (leaflet NP46 published in April 1989 and amended 1 October 1989) and *New Pensions Choices* (leaflets NP40, 41 and 42), for more detailed discussions.

1.2 STATE PROVISION: GUIDE

1.2.1 The State retirement pension: benefits and entitlement

1.2.1.1 Claiming and enhancing the State retirement pension

Whilst a claim can be backdated for a limited period[2], a claim for the State retirement pension should be made during the four months leading up to retirement. The DSS will usually contact the claimant four months before retirement with the relevant claim form.

Category A and B pensions are contributory; Category A being based upon one's own National Insurance contributions and Category B upon the contributions of one's spouse. One person may not claim both pensions but may elect to take that which is the more favourable.

Category C and D pensions are non-contributory and are paid at a lower rate than Category A or the higher rate Category B pensions. These pensions cater for people who have not built up sufficient contributions for a Category A pension or do not have a spouse's contributions to rely upon for a category B pension.

It is possible to enhance the flat-rate Category A or B retirement pension together with any graduated retirement benefit or SERPS, by electing not to receive one's pension for a period of up to five years, even though one is entitled to do so. A statutory formula governs the level of enhancement[3]. In certain circumstances, widows and widowers can take advantage of their former spouses' enhanced benefits[4].

Details of current weekly rates of benefit (as at 6 April 1992) are given in Table 1. These figures represent the maximum benefit available; the amount paid to a claimant may well be reduced if that claimant does not fully satisfy the contribution conditions. There are two main conditions for entitlement to a flat-rate category of pension. The first is that the claimant has reached 'pensionable age': this is defined as 60 for women and 65 for men[5]. The second condition is that the claimant has made (or has been credited with) sufficient National Insurance contributions throughout his or her working life (usually interpreted as 44 years for a woman and 49 years for a man but varying dependent upon an individual's circumstances)[6].

1.2.1.2 Category A pension

The flat-rate pension

A claimant must have paid a sufficient *amount* of contribution for a sufficient *period*. In very broad terms, a claimant must have paid the relevant class of National Insurance contributions at the proper rate for the period of a year (or have paid 50 flat-rate weekly contributions before 6 April 1975) at some point during his or her working life. In order to obtain the maximum flat-rate benefit, this level of contribution must have been maintained by the claimant for approximately 90 per cent of his or her working life. There is a sliding scale of benefit available for claimants who have not fully satisfied the contribution conditions but the scale will not cater for reductions below 25 per cent of the full rate[7].

In certain circumstances, claimants may be credited with contributions even though they have not in fact paid them. There are detailed rules for those whose National Insurance contribution records have been affected by unemployment, sickness, invalidity, disablement or home responsibilities (the latter includes caring for a child under the age of 16, for a person receiving an attendance allowance or for an elderly person)[8]. An important additional category of claimants, who are deemed to have satisfied the contribution requirements, comprises former spouses (where the marriage has been ended by death or divorce) of fully paid-up contributors[9]. This is considered at greater length at **1.3**.

Graduated retirement benefit

Graduated retirement benefit (GRB) was introduced in 1961 by the National Insurance Act 1959. It was discontinued in 1975. GRB was acquired by those paying an amount additional to the flat-rate Class 1 contributions. The system worked on the basis that one unit of GRB would be acquired for a certain level of contribution (£9.00 for a woman and £7.50 for a man). The present unit rate is included in Table 1.

As with the flat-rate benefit, widows and widowers are entitled to rely upon their late spouses' contributions towards GRB to claim the benefit for themselves[10].

Additional pension or State earnings-related pension scheme

State earnings-related pension scheme (SERPS) was introduced in 1978 by the Social Security Pensions Act 1975. The scheme is still in force although the benefits available to claimants will progressively be reduced in the period from 2000 to 2010, by which time the pension will be reduced to 80 per cent of its present value in real terms.

In certain circumstances, a widow or widower may be entitled to rely upon his or her former spouse's SERPS contribution to claim this additional pension (or part thereof) for himself or herself[11]. A widow or widower would have to establish that his or her late spouse died on or after the 6 April 1979 and had satisfied the employee National Insurance contribution conditions. Anything which the late spouse has earned (and in respect of which the appropriate employee National Insurance contributions have been paid) over and above the 'qualifying level' (at least 52 times the lower earnings limit in each tax year) will help to establish entitlement to the additional pension.

Demographic changes, in particular the swelling pensioner population, have encouraged the Government to cut the value of benefits under SERPS. There is in fact no State 'pension fund' built up by National Insurance contributions over the years. Contributions currently made by the working population are immediately redistributed as payments to the pensioner population.

Class 1 National Insurance contributions paid by employees on earnings between the lower and upper earnings limits count as contributions towards SERPS. The aim of the scheme is to provide a claimant with a pension of 25 per cent of 'average revalued earnings' (a type of inflation-proofing, calculated according to a statutory formula) based upon that claimant's average earnings throughout his or her working life. From the second decade of the 21st century that percentage will have decreased to 20 per cent of average revalued earnings. One reduction in the pension has already been made. The level of a pension payable under SERPS was originally calculated on the basis of a percentage of the claimant's *best* 20 years of earnings since the system began; from 6 April 1988 the calculation has been based upon the claimant's earnings throughout the whole of his or her working life, thus reducing the amount of the pension.

As a result of the increased pressure upon the scheme, the Government has in recent years encouraged employees to 'contract out' of SERPS – to give up entitlement to benefits under SERPS in return for benefits provided under their own occupational or personal pension scheme[12]. The Government has encouraged contracting out by offering various contribution incentives.

1.2.1.3 Category B pension

The benefits available under a Category B pension and the contribution conditions to be satisfied by the claimant vary depending upon whether the claimant is a married woman, widow or widower[13].

Married women

A Category B pension for a married woman is paid at the lower rate (see Table 1), but may be increased to take account of any enhancement earned by the woman's husband.

Contribution conditions have to be satisfied by the claimant's husband and will be assessed on the husband's eligibility to receive a Category A pension in his own right. A woman must reach retirement age before becoming entitled to this pension.

Widow

A widow's Category B pension is paid at the higher rate (see Table 1). Eligibility is dependent upon the claimant reaching retirement age and being able to demonstrate that her late husband had made sufficient contributions towards his own Category A pension.

If a widow can establish eligibility for a Category B pension, the benefit is paid indefinitely and does not cease if she either remarries (provided the remarriage took place after 4 April 1971) or cohabits with another man as his wife.

Widower

The benefit is payable at the higher rate (see Table 1). Eligibility depends upon the widower reaching retirement age and demonstrating that his late wife's contributions towards her own Category A pension were sufficient to entitle him to a Category B pension. Once a widower is eligible for this pension, the benefit continues even if he remarries or cohabits with another woman as her husband.

1.2.1.4 Category C pension

Both Category C and Category D pensions are non-contributory. Eligibility depends upon the claimant satisfying age and residence conditions.

A Category C pension is paid at the lower rate (see Table 1) if the claimant is a married woman and special rules apply to widows claiming this pension who are unable to establish eligibility for a Category A or Category B pension[14].

1.2.1.5 Category D pension

The benefit payable under this pension is not reduced for married women but a claimant must establish, in addition to satisfying the residence conditions laid down, that he or she has attained the age of 80.

1.2.1.6 Other benefits

There is an 'age addition' of £0.25 per week for recipients of, inter alia, the State retirement pension, widowed mother's allowance and widow's pension, who have reached the age of 80.

A Christmas bonus is available for recipients of, inter alia, the State retirement pension, widowed mother's allowance and widow's pension. The Christmas bonus is £10 and is paid tax free.

1.2.2 Widow's benefits

1.2.2.1 The concept of widowhood

A woman is a widow only if she was married to the deceased at the date of his death; it does not matter if the parties were separated or even if a decree nisi of divorce had been pronounced but a divorced woman cannot be the widow of her former spouse.

Specific rules apply to void, voidable and polygamous marriages[15].

All widow's benefits cease if a widow remarries. The effect of cohabitation with another man as his wife is less devastating; although a widow's payment will not be made for a widow cohabiting with another man at the date of her husband's death (and the benefit will not be paid to her if she subsequently ceases cohabitation) payment of widowed mother's allowance and widow's pension is merely suspended during a period of cohabitation[16].

'Cohabitation' is not defined in any of the regulations but broadly the adjudication officer (on whom the burden of proof rests) will have to establish that the parties can, taking into account the manner in which they arrange their financial affairs, social life, sexual relationship, etc, be properly considered to have a quasi-matrimonial relationship.

1.2.2.2 Benefits and entitlement

Contributory benefits comprise the widow's payment, widowed mother's allowance and widow's pension. There may also be entitlement to non-contributory widow's benefits and, in the case of certain claims made before 10 April 1990, there may be entitlement to industrial death benefit.

Widow's payment

The widow's payment consists of one lump sum of £1000. The widow must show that she is entitled to the payment by demonstrating that requirements relating to her age and her late husband's contribution record are complied with and that she has made the claim within 12 months of her husband's death **[17]**.

The contribution requirements are fairly generous; the husband must have actually paid, in any one tax year before his death, the relevant Class 1, 2 or 3 contributions or have died as a result of an industrial injury or disease. As far as age is concerned, the claimant must have been under the age of 60 when her husband died or, if over the age of 60, able to demonstrate that her husband was ineligible for a Category A retirement pension when he died (due to age, inadequate contributions or deferment).

Widowed mother's allowance

Widowed mother's allowance consists of a weekly benefit (see Table 1). Any pension payable under SERPS earned by the widow's late husband (provided he died after 5 April 1989) may be added to the basic weekly amount. As with the State retirement pension, it is possible to receive less than the standard amount if the widow's late husband did not fully comply with the entitlement conditions.

A widow's eligibility for this allowance depends upon her late husband's contribution record and upon her being responsible for the care of at least one 'qualifying child' living with her at the relevant time[18]. Broadly, the benefit is aimed at those widows left with child care responsibilities.

Widow's pension

This pension is aimed at women who are either widowed when they are at least 45 years of age or are aged 45 when their child care responsibilities (covered by the widowed mother's allowance) come to an end.

Eligibility depends upon the claimant's age at the relevant date and upon her late husband's contribution record. The rate of benefit can be depressed by up to 70 per cent; a deduction of 7 per cent is made from the standard rate for each year that the widow is under the age of 55 when she becomes entitled to the pension. This percentage does not increase but remains fixed throughout the period of a claim which automatically ends when the widow attains the age of 65. At that point it is assumed that the widow will go on to claim the relevant Class A or Class B retirement pension (which she may have chosen to enhance by electing to postpone her claim until she reaches the age of 65).

Non-contributory widow's benefits

The non-contributory scheme acts as a safety net for those (inevitably elderly) widows who are unable to establish that their late husband satisfied the contribution conditions. For example, benefits are available on a non-contributory basis if a widow can establish that her husband was aged 65 or over on 5 July 1948 and that he was at some time eligible for a Category C retirement pension or if he died before 2 November 1979 and satisfied the residence conditions for the Category C pension.

Industrial death benefit

From 10 April 1990, industrial death benefit is no longer claimable by a widow whose husband has died as a result of an industrial accident or disease. Instead, the husband will be deemed to have complied with the contribution conditions for all widow's benefits and the widow has to demonstrate only that she satisfied the additional entitlement conditions (ie those relating to her age at the date of her husband's death). Detailed rules still apply to a widow claiming under the old industrial death benefit scheme and whose husband died prior to 11 April 1988[19].

1.3 THE EFFECT OF DIVORCE UPON ENTITLEMENT

There are two useful leaflets prepared by the DSS dealing with the effect on a woman's National Insurance position of widowhood (leaflet NI 51) and divorce (leaflet NI 95).

1.3.1 Category A

1.3.1.1 The flat-rate pension

By virtue of s 20 of the Social Security Pensions Act 1975, a divorced claimant may elect to have her record of contributions substituted by that of the former spouse, if such a substitution would be in her interest. A divorced claimant may elect to have the substitution operate either from the beginning of her working life until the date the marriage ended or simply for the period of the marriage itself.

Where a divorced claimant has been married more than once, her ability to elect for such a substitution will apply only to her last spouse's contribution record. Remarriage destroys a claim for this pension based upon the contributions of a previously divorced (or deceased) spouse.

These rules apply equally to widows and widowers.

Where on divorce both parties are over retirement age and where one party (usually the husband) receives the full Category A pension, the wife receiving the lower-rate Category B pension, the wife would be able to claim the full Category A pension from the date of divorce. She would not, however, be able to claim any additional pension based upon her former husband's contribution to SERPS.

Graduated retirement benefit

There is no provision for the use of a former spouse's record of contribution to assist a divorced person to claim this benefit. Any claim under the GRB rule would have to be made upon the claimant's own record. A claimant may, therefore, be denied access to this benefit from which he or she would otherwise have benefited indirectly as a result of his or her spouse making the appropriate claim had they remained married.

The additional pension or State earnings-related pension scheme

There is no provision for the use of a former spouse's record of contributions to assist a divorced claimant to claim this benefit. Any claim under SERPS would have to be based on the claimant's own record.

1.3.2 Category B pension

Married women, widows and widowers may be able to establish their entitlement to a Category B pension by relying upon the contribution record of their spouse or deceased spouse. Divorced pensioners are *not* able to demonstrate eligibility based upon their former spouse's contribution record and this pension is not available to them.

1.3.3 Category C and D pensions

Eligibility for Category C and D pensions depends upon the claimant satisfying the entitlement conditions (which are non-contributory) for herself. Divorce may even enhance a Category C pension claim by a woman who, as a divorcee, will be paid at the higher rate while she remains unmarried.

1.3.4 Other benefits

Entitlement to the age addition depends upon the claimant reaching 80; the claimant is not able to rely upon anybody else satisfying the condition.

A Christmas bonus is payable to a claimant in her own right provided she is claiming the appropriate benefit.

1.3.5 Widow's benefits

A divorced woman will never be regarded as the widow of a man from whom she is divorced. The entitlement conditions for widow's benefits will, therefore, never be satisfied in respect of that former spouse. The effect of divorce will be that the woman loses all State widow's benefits in respect of that former husband.

NOTES

1. Social Security Act 1989, s 7(1) and Sch 9.
2. Social Security (Claims and Payments) Regulations 1987, regs 15 and 19.
3. Social Security Pensions Act 1975, Sch 1, paras 1 and 2 (as amended by the Social Security Act 1989, s 7(4) and Sch 1, para 3).
4. Social Security Pensions Act 1975, s 1(4) (as amended by Social Security Act 1989, s 7(4), Sch 1).
5. Social Security Act 1975, s 27(1).
6. Social Security Act 1975, Sch 3 para 5 (as amended by Social Security Pensions Act 1975, s 19).
7. Social Security (Widow's Benefit and Retirement Pension) Regulations 1979, reg 2(1).
8. Social Security Pensions (Home Responsibilities and Miscellaneous Amendments) Regulations 1978.
9. Social Security Pensions Act 1975, s 20.
10. National Insurance Act 1965, s 37 (kept in force by Social Security (Graduated Retirement Benefit) (No 2) Regulations 1978, Sch 1).
11. Social Security Pensions Act 1975, s 9(3) and Social Security (Maximum Additional Component) Regulations 1978.
12. Social Security Act 1986, s 66, Sch 6.
13. Social Security Act 1975, s 29, Sch 3, para 10 and Sch 4.
14. Social Security (Widow's Benefit and Retirement Pension) Regulations 1979, regs 11(1), 12, 13(2) and 14(1).
15. Decisions of the National Insurance and Social Security Commissioner, R(G) 2/63 and R(G) 1/73 and Social Security and Family Allowances (Polygamous Marriages) Regulations 1975.
16. Social Security Act 1975, ss 25(3) and 26(3).
17. Social Security Act 1975, s 24 (as amended by Social Security Act 1986, Sch 3 and Social Security (Widow's Benefit and Retirement Pension) Regulations 1979, reg 16).
18. Social Security Act 1975, s 26(2).
19. Social Security Act 1975, s 67 (as amended by Social Security Act 1986, Social Security Act 1988, and Social Security (General Benefits) Regulations 1982, reg 23).

- unapproved schemes and arrangements (see **2.7**): schemes and other arrangements established outside Inland Revenue supervision and control, including partner's annuities.

2.2 STATUTORY PENSION SCHEMES

Statutory pension schemes are government-funded and administered schemes set up for public sector employees. They are established by Act of Parliament (or by statutory instrument authorised by Act of Parliament) and their detailed provisions are therefore found in legislation rather than in trust deeds and rules. There are statutory schemes for all the following public sector employees:

Civil Servants
Local Government Employees
Teachers
NHS Employees
Police
Firemen
University Employees
Armed Services
The Judiciary.

Other categories of public sector employees (for example, Post Office workers, British Coal employees and British Rail employees) are covered by pension schemes which bear more similarity to conventional occupational pension schemes than to statutory schemes. These public sector workers have pension schemes governed by trust deeds and rules, even though the authority for their establishment is in statute or statutory instrument. They are not therefore dealt with here but are dealt with under occupational pension schemes (see **2.3**). The privatised industries also have their own private occupational pension schemes.

The distinguishing characteristic of statutory pension schemes is that they are, in the main, unfunded. Benefits are paid out of the current assets of the employer rather than out of a separate pension fund.

2.2.1 Benefits

Most schemes provide for payment of an annual pension of one-eightieth of the employee's final annual salary for each year of his pensionable service and for a tax-free cash sum of three times the pension (or sometimes a tax-free cash sum broadly equivalent to the final year's salary).

It is common for death benefits to be one year's pay or the lump sum retirement benefit which would have been paid had the member retired due to ill health at the time he died. Benefits for death during retirement are significantly reduced.

The widow's pension is usually full pay for the first three months of widowhood in the case of death in service, or full pension for that three months if the member has already retired, followed by a continuing pension during her lifetime. The widow's pension where the member's death occurs during retirement is usually roughly half the member's actual pension.

Beyond that it is difficult to generalise. Where any detailed information about benefits available under a scheme is required, reference should be made to the statute or statutory instrument for the scheme concerned where the full scheme rules will be set out.

All the statutory schemes publish booklets summarising the main provisions, although these booklets sometimes sacrifice detail for brevity.

The position of the armed forces is considered separately at **4.8**.

2.3 OCCUPATIONAL PENSION SCHEMES

Occupational pension schemes are schemes established by an employer or group of employers to provide pension benefits for employees and their dependants on retirement or death in service. They vary enormously in size and are found across the spectrum of different types of business, from the public sector employers and large industrial companies to the small professional practice. Directors with more than a 20 per cent interest in a company are excluded from membership of that company's occupational pension scheme, and benefits for them are more commonly provided in small self-administered schemes (see **2.4**).

The term 'occupational pension scheme' can be used as a general term to describe any scheme provided by employers for employees. In this chapter, however, it is used to describe the traditional type of scheme established by trust deed and rules.

The essential source of detailed information about these schemes is the *Inland Revenue Practice Notes* 'Occupational Pension Schemes' (IR12, 1991).

2.3.1 Structure and management

An occupational pension scheme is established by the employer setting up a trust and appointing trustees to administer the funds. The trust deed and accompanying rules set out the scheme rules for administration of the scheme, investment of funds, eligibility to join and the benefits payable to members. All questions about benefits are therefore addressed to the trustees of the scheme. Most members of larger schemes are provided with a scheme booklet which sets out a simple version of these rules.

To enable both employer and employee to gain valuable tax reliefs on contributions and benefits, the trust deed and rules must be approved by the PSO. The constitution and management of these schemes is therefore strictly controlled.

Since 6 April 1988, employers have no longer been able to make it a condition of employment that an employee joins an occupational pension scheme. Many employees now choose not to belong to their employer's scheme. Some choose to save money by making no pension provision at all; others may take out personal pension schemes (see **2.6**).

2.3.2 Investment of funds

The trustees of a scheme may invest the funds belonging to the scheme in chosen investments (subject to statutory control) or may place the funds with an insurance company to invest for them.

Approved schemes enjoy very significant concessions on the investment of funds. Most importantly, investment income is free from income tax and disposals are free from capital gains tax.

2.3.3 Contributions and the earnings cap

Employers must contribute to occupational pension schemes and in many schemes the employer makes a larger contribution than the employee. Whether or not the employee contributes and how much he contributes depends on the terms of the scheme and his agreement with his employer.

It is often a condition of scheme membership for the employee to contribute a fixed percentage (say five per cent) of his gross earnings. The employee may have the opportunity to make additional voluntary contributions (AVCs). Under current rules, an employee's total contributions must not exceed 15 per cent of his gross earnings in order to obtain income tax relief.

There is an upper limit of contributions for some well-paid employees known as the 'earnings cap'. The earnings cap applies only to those who became members of an existing approved scheme after 1 June 1989, or to members of new schemes established after 14 March 1989. In the 1992/93 tax year, 15 per cent of income up to a maximum limit of income of £75,000 per annum can be contributed and still qualify for tax relief (the upper limit goes up each year in line with the RPI). Higher contributions can be made but the employee will not get tax relief on them.

2.3.4 Normal retirement date

Members of an occupational pension scheme cannot usually retire and receive benefits until they reach the retirement date specified in the trust deed and rules. Although the retirement date is usually between 60 and 65, the Inland Revenue may approve retirement dates as early as age 50. The ability to provide different retirement ages for men and women has been in doubt since the decision of the European Court of Justice in the case of *Barber v Guardian Royal Exchange* (Case No C-262/88) and the position remains unclear. Under the so-called Maastricht Protocol, Article 119 of the Treaty of Rome has been amended so that equal treatment will apply only in respect of rights accrued after 17 May 1990. However, the Protocol has not as yet been ratified by all member States. The position will be considered later this year by the European Court of Justice in *Re Coloroll*. Lower retirement dates are allowed by the Inland Revenue for schemes applying to persons in certain special occupations (eg sportsmen, air pilots and dancers).

The trust deed and rules will usually require the employer to consent to early retirement in these circumstances. Early retirement may also be available either voluntarily or on grounds of incapacity due to ill health.

2.3.5 Leaving employment: transfers

When the member leaves the relevant employment or scheme, most schemes now provide the following alternatives:

(a) a refund of the employee's own contributions, sometimes with interest (if the employee has less than two years' service with the employer);
(b) a transfer of benefits to the new employer's scheme;
(c) a transfer of benefits to a personal pension scheme (transfers to retirement annuity contracts are not allowed);
(d) preservation of benefits in the occupational pension scheme until the employee's retirement date.

2.3.6 Source of pension

The pension may be paid out of the assets held by the scheme (more usual in larger schemes). Alternatively, on retirement, an annuity may be purchased from an insurance company which will pay the lump sum and other pension benefits to the pensioner and/or his dependants over the years that follow.

2.3.7 Benefits on retirement

The method of calculating benefits under an occupational pension scheme will usually be set out in the scheme rules.

Traditionally, occupational pension schemes have provided pensions based on a calculation involving final salary (a final salary scheme). The maximum pension benefit which can be provided for members of schemes which came into existence before 14 March 1989, where the members joined the scheme before 1 June 1989, is two-thirds of the member's final pensionable earnings.

Money purchase schemes based on the investment performance of units purchased by the pension scheme for the employee are now more common.

Benefits on early retirement are usually more generous if an employee retires due to ill-health rather than by choice.

2.3.7.1 Continuing pension

The main benefit payable to an employee is the continuing pension payable for the rest of his life. The Social Security Act 1990 provides that all pensions must have some form of indexation to keep pace with inflation and cannot remain fixed. This provision is not yet in force. Many schemes already provide for different methods of indexing benefits and for different levels of increase.

The pension received is taxed as if it were the earned income of the pensioner.

2.3.7.2 Lump sum

On retirement (or in anticipation of retirement), the trustees or the insurance company administering the fund for the trustees will provide a statement showing how much of the fund can be taken as a lump sum. The process of taking a lump sum in lieu of part of a continuing pension is known as commutation.

A lump sum taken as a commutation of pension entitlement is tax free in the hands of the recipient. Under current Inland Revenue rules for approved schemes, the maximum lump sum which can be taken is whichever is the greater of:

(a) three-eightieths of final remuneration for each year of service up to 40 years; and
(b) 2.25 times the amount that the pension would be if no lump sum were taken.

Under schemes established before 14 March 1989 where the member joined before 1 June 1989, the usual limit is up to 1.5 times the member's final salary after more than 20 years' service, with lower amounts for shorter periods of service.

The figures quoted here are the maxima allowed by the Inland Revenue; the individual rules of the scheme must be checked and will often provide for a lower level of lump sum payment.

2.3.7.3 Interrelation with State pensions

A person who receives a pension under an occupational pension scheme will still receive a basic State retirement pension but will receive a State earnings-related pension only if the scheme is not contracted out of SERPS. Most occupational pension schemes are contracted out. Where the scheme is contracted out, it is obliged to provide the employee with a guaranteed minimum pension instead of a pension under SERPS. The employee is therefore guaranteed not to receive less than he would have received if he had not contracted out of SERPS.

Within contracted-out schemes, the employer's promise to provide a guaranteed minimum pension creates a scheme within a scheme. The body of separate rights attaching to GMPs are called 'protected rights' and are the subject of special rules, particularly on transfers to other schemes.

2.3.8 Dependant's benefits

2.3.8.1 Death in retirement

The trust deed and rules of occupational pension schemes commonly provide for a continuing pension (usually about half the level of the member's pension) to be paid to a widow or widower, but not to a former spouse. A pension scheme may, however, where there is no widow or widower (or, occasionally, in addition to making a payment to a widow or widower), provide a pension payable to 'dependants', as defined in the trust deed and rules. Lump sum payments on death in retirement are rare and limited.

Benefits pass outside the estate of the deceased and not by will; they are therefore free from inheritance tax. Where benefits are payable to dependants, the choice of dependant or dependants to benefit normally lies with the trustees. The trustees are likely to be influenced in their decision by a statement, letter of expression of wish or 'nomination' provided before death by a member but they may also conduct their own investigations as to appropriate beneficiaries.

2.3.8.2 Death in service

On death in service, the scheme may provide all or any of the following:

(a) a lump sum of up to four times the member's final remuneration at date of death;
(b) up to two-thirds of the pension which the member would have received had he survived to usual retirement age;
(c) a refund of contributions paid.

The maximum lump sum death-in-service benefit for members subject to an earnings cap (see **2.3.3**) is £300,000 for 1992/93.

The lump sum or returned contributions may be paid to the member's estate or nominated beneficiary, or distributed at the discretion of the trustees. A continuing pension may be payable to a widow, widower or dependant. Benefits pass outside the estate of the deceased and are not subject to inheritance tax.

2.4 SMALL SELF-ADMINISTERED SCHEMES

Until 1973, directors with a 20 per cent or greater interest in their company could not be members of their company's occupational pension scheme. They had to rely, therefore, on private provision in the form of a retirement annuity contract. Although the Finance Act 1973 permitted these directors to become members of company schemes, s 15 of the Act introduced a new type of company scheme, specifically designed for the '20 per cent director'. These are known as small self-administered schemes.

These schemes have achieved a certain notoriety since they allow a measure of freedom of investment which would be unusual in the world of the standard occupational or personal pension scheme. They are, however, quite properly and widely used by directors of small companies to combine the provision of retirement benefits with an ability to use funds invested in an effective manner.

2.4.1 Structure and management

The schemes must be established by the company through a trust deed and rules, for which PSO approval is required. The number of members is normally limited to 12 or less; all the members must be trustees of the scheme and directors of the company. PSO rules require the appointment of a 'Pensioner Trustee', a person approved by the PSO from outside the company to notify the PSO of any intention to wind the scheme up early and distribute assets.

2.4.2 Investment of funds

The peculiarity of small, self-administered schemes is that funds can be invested in a wider range of assets than is the case with any other type of approved scheme. For example, such schemes can buy real property from or for the company, buy the company's shares, and lend money to the company. Schemes may also invest in more conventional assets such as insurance policies, and many do.

Actuarial reports on investment have to be submitted by the trustees to the PSO every three years, and these provide a valuable source of information about the scheme on discovery. Information about investment rules is contained in the Social Security Act 1990 and the Occupational Pension Schemes (Investment of Schemes Resources) Regulations 1992, which have placed new restrictions on investment. Most importantly, trustees can no longer invest more than five per cent of the scheme's resources in employer-related investments.

2.4.3 Contributions

Both the company and the individual director may make contributions to the scheme's fund. The purpose of small self-administered schemes is often to maximise the tax-effectiveness of the company's contributions for members. The level of contribution may be set out in the trust deed and rules but more often there will be a separate agreement between the individual director and the company about what contributions each will make. The limit for tax-free contributions by individual directors is 15 per cent of gross earnings, but not subject to the maximum income limit or 'earnings cap'. Contributions can be made regularly or on a 'one-off' basis, and the scheme rules will often provide for payment of AVCs (see Glossary).

Although it is theoretically possible for these schemes to be contracted out, in practice they never are.

2.4.4 Normal retirement date

A small self-administered scheme must specify a normal retirement date. The rules as to the date which may be specified are the same as those applying to occupational pension schemes (see **2.3.4**), but in a small self-administered scheme the flexibility to agree on earlier or later retirement date is of particular significance. Most importantly, benefits may continue to accrue up to age 70 and beyond.

2.4.5 Benefits on retirement

As the member approaches his retirement date, the trustees must take steps to dispose of assets to make sure that there is sufficient cash to pay benefits to the retiring director. The trustees are under an obligation to pay benefits from this retirement date, and to secure the payment of those benefits by purchasing an annuity within five years of the retirement of the director.

Benefits will be a combination of:

(a) a tax-free lump sum of up to one and a half times final annual salary (which is calculated by reference to any three consecutive years prior to retirement date);
(b) a continuing pension of up to two-thirds of final salary.

2.4.6 Benefits on death in service

Benefits will be any of (or a combination of):

(a) a widow's or dependant's pension;
(b) a tax-free lump sum of up to four times final salary;
(c) return of contributions.

These benefits pass outside the members' estate for inheritance tax purposes and may be paid to named beneficiaries or at the discretion of the remaining trustees, whose discretion may be influenced by the member's nomination before death.

2.5 PERSONAL PENSION SCHEMES

2.5.1 Introduction

The essence of personal pension schemes is flexibility and mobility. Personal pensions have been available since 1 July 1988; the governing legislation is in the Income and Corporation Taxes Act 1988, Chapter IV, ss 630 to 655. Personal pensions were designed to replace retirement annuity contracts which were intended for the self-employed, but were aimed at certain employees as well as the self-employed. They bear many similarities to retirement annuity contracts but there are important differences, most significantly:

(a) employers can contribute to personal pension schemes. They are therefore designed for employees as well as the self-employed. Employers cannot contribute to retirement annuity contracts;
(b) tax relief is available at source for contributions to personal pension schemes by employees. For retirement annuity contracts, tax relief is available only retrospectively;
(c) the first payment of pension under a personal pension scheme may be made between the ages of 50 and 75, compared with 60 as the starting date for retirement annuity contracts;
(d) personal pensions can be used to contract out of SERPS so that employees qualify for reduced national insurance contributions; retirement annuity contracts cannot be used in this way;
(e) personal pensions are subject to the 'earnings cap' for high earners; retirement annuity contracts are not;
(f) a fixed percentage of 25 per cent of the fund arising under a personal pension scheme is available as a tax-free lump sum on retirement; the lump sum available under a retirement annuity contract is assessed by reference to a more complex calculation.

2.5.2 Eligibility

In addition to the self-employed, the following categories of employees are eligible to take out personal pensions:

(a) employees in non-pensionable employment;
(b) employees who are in pensionable employment but who have decided not to join their employer's pension scheme or are ineligible to do so; and
(c) employees who are members of an approved occupational scheme in cases where the scheme provides only lump sum death-in-service benefits and/or a pension for a surviving spouse or dependant (there are many industry-wide approved schemes providing basic life cover and widow's and dependants' benefits for employees in industries where employees are traditionally mobile, eg the construction, shopfitting and car industries).

2.5.3 Structure and management

Personal pension schemes are taken out as a contract between an individual and a provider of pensions – usually an insurance company, although it may be a friendly society, bank, building society or unit trust company. The scheme rules are set out in the individual's policy document.

2.5.4 Investment of funds

Funds are invested by the insurance company on behalf of the individual policyholder. The range of investments allowed is wider than for occupational pension schemes.

2.5.5 Contributions and the earnings cap

Both employer and employee may contribute; the amount to be contributed by the employer will depend on the terms of employment. Contributions can be paid as regular instalments or one-off payments.

The maximum total contribution which can be made depends upon the member's age and his net relevant earnings.

Members who established new personal pension schemes after 14 March 1989, or who joined an existing (group) personal pension scheme after 1 June 1989, are limited to contributions based on net relevant earnings. The maximum allowable contributions are:

Up to age 35:	17.5 per cent
Between the ages 36 and 45:	20 per cent
Between the ages 46 and 50:	25 per cent
Between the ages 51 and 55:	30 per cent
Between the ages 56 and 60:	35 per cent
Over the age of 60:	40 per cent.

The earnings cap for net relevant earnings in the 1992/93 tax year is £75,000.

Contributions must be made from earned income; unearned income or capital does not qualify as net relevant earnings.

2.5.6 Contracting out

There are many examples of personal pension schemes established after July 1988 solely to receive the benefit of 'minimum contributions' payable by the DSS direct to the trustees of 'contracted out' money purchase schemes. Minimum contributions consist of a payment by the DSS of:

(a) the partial rebate of National Insurance contributions resulting from the decision to contract out of SERPS; and
(b) an incentive payment, payable for five years from 6 April 1987 to 1993 of two per cent of the employee's earnings between the lower and upper earnings levels for NI purposes.

Employers pay full-rate National Insurance contributions for all employees, whether or not they are contracted out. The DSS then calculates from the earnings information provided in the employers' year end tax return what minimum contribution is due in respect of each employee. Following the end of each tax year the DSS pays the trustees of such plans the relevant National Insurance rebate, together with any incentive payment. Basic rate tax relief is also added to the employee's portion of the National Insurance rebate.

2.5.7 Normal retirement age

Benefits can be drawn from a retirement age between 50 and 75 except in cases of special occupations and permanent incapacity, in which case an earlier retirement age may be allowed. The benefits may be drawn even if the individual continues to work, although the individual may incur a higher income tax liability by doing so.

2.5.8 Benefits on retirement and death

On retirement, at the chosen date, the individual will be entitled to a continuing pension and will usually be able to opt for a lump sum. Taking the lump sum will reduce the amount of the continuing pension payable.

Since personal pension schemes are money purchase schemes, benefits are based on the amount of contributions and the investment performance of the fund and not final salary.

2.5.8.1 Lump sum

The amount of the tax-free lump sum which can be taken from a personal pension depends on whether the scheme was established before or after 27 July 1989. For personal pension schemes established before 27 July 1989, the maximum amount of the tax-free lump sum which can be taken is 25 per cent of the total fund, excluding that part of the fund established to provide widows' or dependants' benefits. For schemes established after 27 July 1989, the maximum tax-free lump sum is 25 per cent of the total fund, excluding that part of the fund which represents protected rights. No lump sum can be paid in relation to protected rights, nor can such benefits be paid earlier than age 60 or 65.

2.5.8.2 Continuing pension

Insurance companies offer a wide range of options for the method of payment of the continuing pension. The method chosen will affect the amount paid. The company may offer payment in advance or in arrears; it may also offer different levels of inflation proofing. Commonly, pensions escalate at a fixed rate of five per cent per annum.

2.5.8.3 Protected rights

Personal pension benefits derived from minimum contributions (see **2.5.6**) are treated as 'protected rights', because they represent the guaranteed minimum pension benefits which would otherwise have been paid to the member under SERPS. Protected pension rights may not be taken from personal pension schemes until the normal State retirement age. They must also be taken in a prescribed form, ie as a pension which increases at three per cent per annum compound, together with a compulsory pension of 50 per cent of the member's pension for the surviving spouse in circumstances where the member dies while in receipt of a protected rights pension. The member is not able to commute any part of his protected rights pension benefits for a tax-free lump sum payment.

2.5.9 Benefits for dependants

The benefits available both on death in service and during retirement vary widely and reference should be made to the provisions of the scheme concerned.

Benefits on death before retirement are often limited to a return of contributions (with or without interest) or a return of the accumulated fund. Many policies incorporate an element of life cover, in which case an additional capital sum will be payable.

Continuing payment of a pension to dependants is only available on death during retirement.

Benefits on death can be written in trust for dependants. The policyholder can usually direct that the fund should be paid to a named beneficiary on his death, or that the fund should be paid to a trustee with a discretion to appoint the fund to one or more beneficiaries. The fund therefore passes outside the estate for Inheritance Tax purposes. There are no restrictions on the class of potential beneficiaries and so an adult child or ex-wife can be named.

2.5.10 Transfers

Personal pension schemes can accept funds transferred from all other types of approved pension scheme.

2.6 RETIREMENT ANNUITY CONTRACTS: 'SECTION 226 POLICIES'

Until 1 July 1988 the only type of individual pension scheme available was a retirement annuity contract, used largely to provide retirement benefits for the self-employed. These schemes, commonly known as 'section 226 policies', can no longer be taken out since they have been replaced by personal pension schemes. Many retirement annuity contracts taken out before 1 July 1988 are, however, still in existence and so an understanding of both types of scheme is required.

Retirement annuity contracts were designed for the self-employed and were not available to employees who were members of occupational pension schemes, although they were available to employees who were not members of such a scheme. They were widely used by those with a combination of salaried employment and private earnings. For example, doctors with an NHS and a private practice might use a section 226 policy to make retirement provision from the private element of their earnings.

The legislation concerning retirement annuity contracts was formerly contained in the Income and Corporation Taxes Act 1970, ss 226 to 228; the provisions are now contained in the Income and Corporation Taxes Act 1988, ss 618 to 629.

2.6.1 Structure and management

Retirement annuity contracts are contracts between an individual and an insurance company for the insurance company to provide benefits on retirement or death for that individual or his dependants. The rules are set out in the policy document. The fund is managed by the insurance company for the policyholder.

2.6.2 Investment of funds

Retirement annuity contracts are always money purchase schemes. The contributions are invested with an insurance company under the terms of the contract and the benefits payable at retirement are based on the investment performance of the fund established by the contributions.

2.6.3 Contributions

Although new contracts cannot now be taken out, contributions can still be paid to policies taken out before 1 July 1988. They have the advantage for high earners that the earnings cap, described at **2.5.5**, does not apply. Contributions may be paid as regular instalments or one-off payments.

Contributions must be paid out of 'relevant earnings' and cannot be paid out of unearned income or capital, but the contributions may represent a higher percentage of earnings than is allowed for employees. The percentage which is allowed depends on age; the maximum allowable contributions are:

Up to age 50:	17.5 per cent
Between the ages 51 and 55:	20 per cent
Between the ages 56 and 60:	22.5 per cent
Between the ages 61 and 74:	27.5 per cent

Contributions up to the maximum percentage are excluded from the calculation of the individual's income tax liability.

Retirement annuity contracts cannot be used to contract out of SERPS.

2.6.4 Normal retirement age

Benefits under retirement annuity contracts cannot be taken before the age of 60, other than in the case of death, permanent incapacity due to ill health, or where the policyholder is engaged in some special occupation (such as sportsmen, air pilots or dancers). Under personal pension schemes, benefits may be taken from the age of 50. Funds held in retirement annuity contracts may be transferred to personal pension schemes, thus enabling benefits to be taken earlier.

2.6.5 Benefits on retirement

Having chosen a retirement date between the ages of 60 and 75, the individual will be entitled to payment of a pension when he reaches the retirement age and he may, in addition, elect to take a tax-free lump sum from the fund which has accumulated up to that date. Since these schemes are money purchase schemes, the amount of the benefits is based on the amount of contributions and the investment performance of the fund and not final salary.

2.6.5.1 Lump sum

The maximum lump sum which may be taken involves a calculation which can only realistically be carried out by the insurance company concerned. As a very rough guide this may be in the region of 30 per cent of the total fund: rather more than the 25 per cent available under personal pension schemes.

It is usually advisable for the individual to take the tax-free cash sum, but there is the option to leave it in the fund where it will be used to increase the amount of continuing pension provision.

2.6.5.2 Continuing pension

Insurance companies usually offer a range of options for the method of payment of the pension. The method chosen will affect the amount paid. For example, payment of pension annually in arrear will yield the highest pension; opting for monthly payments in advance, or a pension payable during the joint lives of the individual and his spouse will yield a lower pension. The insurance company may also offer different levels of inflation proofing – commonly, pensions escalate at five per cent per annum.

2.6.5.3 Interrelation with State pension

Since retirement annuity contracts cannot be used to contract out of SERPS, benefits are paid in addition to the State retirement pension and any entitlement under an occupational scheme or SERPS.

2.6.6 Benefits for dependants

The benefits available both on death in service and death during retirement vary widely and reference should be made to the provisions of the individual contract. Benefits on death before retirement are often limited to a return of contributions (with or without interest) or a return of the accumulated fund, together with payment of any cash sum guaranteed by way of life cover. Continuing payment of a pension to dependants is only available on death during retirement.

Retirement benefits cannot be assigned but it is possible for the policyholder to write death benefits in trust for dependants. The policyholder can usually direct that the entire fund should be paid to a single beneficiary immediately on his death, or that the fund should be paid to a trustee who will have a discretion to appoint the fund to one or more of a class of potential beneficiaries.

Death benefits paid out under policies written in trust are free from inheritance tax liability since the payment is to the trustees for beneficiaries rather than to the estate of the policyholder. It is therefore essential for tax-planning purposes that retirement annuity contracts should be written in trust. There are no restrictions on the class of potential beneficiaries, so policies can be written in trust for former wives or adult children.

2.6.7 Transfers

Funds held under retirement annuity contracts can be transferred to personal pension schemes or other retirement annuity contracts. One obvious reason for wishing to transfer benefits to a personal pension scheme would be because benefits could be taken early rather than the member having to wait until age 60.

Retirement annuity contracts cannot accept transfer payments from other pension schemes, apart from other retirement annuity contracts.

2.7 UNAPPROVED SCHEMES AND ARRANGEMENTS

Until the Finance Act 1989, any provision made by any employer to pay retirement benefits to an employee outside Inland Revenue control and approval would have caused approved pension provision for that employee to be invalidated. The Finance Act 1989 allows unapproved and approved schemes to exist alongside each other. Unapproved schemes may now be established by those employers who wish to provide retirement benefits for employees in excess of the benefits allowed under approved schemes – for example to highly paid employees whose earnings are above the earnings cap.

The arrangements may provide for the employer to make an immediate or regular contribution towards the cost of the unapproved benefits to be provided. Alternatively, he may make no immediate payment but ask the employee to accept an undertaking that the pension benefits will be provided on normal retirement or earlier. The tax consequences for both employer and employee of providing unapproved pension benefits by immediate funding, or by an unfunded undertaking are as follows.

(a) Where a company makes a payment to an unapproved retirement benefit scheme, it will receive immediate corporation tax relief, but the employee will be subject to income tax on the amount of the payment at his top rate of income tax as if the payment were earnings. Pension benefits from a funded unapproved scheme are subject to income tax but lump sum benefits are tax free. If properly constituted as a 'sponsored superannuation scheme', death benefits payable under a funded unapproved scheme should not be the subject of inheritance tax.

(b) Where on retirement an employee receives a payment from an unfunded unapproved scheme, whether in the form of a lump sum, or a pension, the company will receive corporation tax relief on the payment and the employee will be subject to income tax on both forms of pension payment. In the case of unfunded, unapproved schemes, any payment of death benefit will be subject to inheritance tax.

It is difficult to generalise about unapproved schemes and arrangements, but it is important to be aware that they may exist.

2.8 PARTNERS' ANNUITIES

Also unapproved but not strictly a form of pension provision are the annuities commonly paid to retiring partners under partnership agreements. These are usually treated by the Inland Revenue as payments for goodwill and, although they provide benefits on retirement, they fall outside pension legislation and revenue control.

In such cases there is no pension scheme, and no contributions to a fund are made by the partnership or the individual partner. It is a purely contractual arrangement to pay further remuneration to a partner after his retirement and neither the partner nor the partnership benefits from the tax concessions available under conventional pension arrangements.

Annuity arrangements are becoming less common since partners increasingly make their own pension arrangements.

CHAPTER 3

INSURANCE FRAMEWORK: LIFE ASSURANCE AND OTHER TYPES OF INSURANCE

3.1 INTRODUCTION

Many of the difficulties encountered with pensions do not arise in the case of life assurance policies. The policies themselves are familiar, both to practitioners and to clients, particularly the endowment policy which is so often used as collateral security for mortgages. Practitioners are also far more familiar with the practical arrangements, both in obtaining information about the value of the policies and the ultimate benefits, and in assigning the benefit of the policies. None the less, for the family law practitioner there are a number of difficulties arising from the limitations on the orders which can be made under MCA 1973.

It should be noted that life assurance policies are 'property' for the purposes of s 24(1)(a) of MCA 1973, and the court is therefore able to order a transfer of such policies from one spouse to the other.

The purpose of this chapter is to give the background to the law relating to life assurance and the requirements for the correct assignment of benefits under such policies. A brief survey of the most important types of policy is also included, as well as life assurance in its various guises. Some consideration is also given to other types of policy which are encountered on family breakdown and which it may be helpful to consider here as part of the range of policies which the practitioner may meet when dealing with the problems of the client and his or her family.

3.2 HOW DOES LIFE ASSURANCE WORK?

3.2.1 What is life assurance?

Life assurance is a contract by which one party (the insurer) undertakes for consideration (the premium) to pay money (the sum assured) to or for the benefit of the other party (the assured) upon the occurrence of a specified event. The objective for the assured is to provide a sum for himself or others in the event of his death.

Strictly speaking, a life *assurance* policy is one under which the beneficiary is *assured* of the benefits at an event certain, for example a specified date or the earlier death of the person whose life is assured. A contingency *insurance* policy is one by which the beneficiary is *insured* against a contingency, which could be death before a particular date or some other event which is not certain.

A life assurance policy is a legal chose in action – that is, part of the group of 'personal rights of property which can only be claimed or enforced by action, and not by taking physical possession' (*Torkington v Magee* [1902] 2 KB 427, per Channell J). The law relating to the assignment of life assurance policies is that governing legal choses in action and is referred to at **3.4.1.1** and **3.4.1.2**.

3.2.2 Who can take out a policy?

The essence of insurance is to protect against possible losses in the future, rather than making a profit through gambling. The Life Assurance Act 1774 requires that a policyholder must have an insurable interest at the time when a contract is made on the life of an assured.

There is no statutory definition of what constitutes an insurable interest, though there is a substantial body of case law on the subject. It is presumed that a person has an unlimited insurable interest in his own life, and that of his spouse. It has been held that the loss is not to be assessed purely on the value of the services which the wife renders (*Wainwright v Bland* (1835) 1 Moo and R 481; *Griffiths v Fleming* [1909] 1 KB 805).

Family law practitioners should be aware that former spouses do not have this unlimited insurable interest. In practice, applications to insure the life of a former spouse will be considered by companies to cover the loss of maintenance, since that is a tangible financial loss, but the point should, none the less, be borne in mind. If the absence of an insurable interest creates difficulties, it is of course open to the former spouse to take out the policy on his or her own life and then assign the policy, but this can only be done by agreement. It is important to be aware of the limitations of MCA 1973: in *Milne v Milne* (1981) FLR 286, the Court of Appeal held that the judge of first instance had been wrong to order a husband to take out an insurance policy: 'In my judgment, such a life insurance policy, although being eminently suitable in the circumstances of this case . . . is not a step that can be ordered by the court' (per Purchas J at p 287). These problems are considered later at **6.5.2**.

It is also important to bear in mind another practical problem in this context: the court cannot order an unwilling party to undergo a medical examination. For example, if a wife wishes to insure the life of her husband to cover maintenance payments, there is nothing a court can do to ensure that the husband submits to the usual examination. The practitioner should avoid any such difficulties when negotiating a settlement by incorporating an appropriate undertaking in any consent order. (A draft undertaking is to be found in the Appendix, precedent 3(c)). The problem cannot always be avoided; the sort of obstructive behaviour which is envisaged is likely to be encountered in contested proceedings rather than where a settlement has been successfully negotiated and it may be that false information will be given by an obstructive husband, thereby resulting in the proposal being declined or accepted on unfavourable terms. In such cases, secured provision might be appropriate as a way of countering such behaviour and safeguarding the position of the person receiving maintenance (see **6.5.4** on survival of claims on death).

It is doubtful whether a child has an insurable interest per se in the life of his parent (*Halford v Kymer* (1830) 10 B & C 724), unless there is a potential financial loss. Such a loss might occur in cases of partnership, or more familiarly in anticipating inheritance tax on the potential death of a parent. Similarly, unless there is some pecuniary interest, a parent has no insurable interest in a child. Although there is no authority on the point, it seems reasonably clear that, on marriage breakdown, there is an insurable interest where there is an obligation to maintain under an agreement or order. Life assurance companies will consider applications made on behalf of children to insure the life of a parent who is paying maintenance to the extent of the payments that would be lost on death.

Insurable interests in real property have been recognised as vesting in both trustees and beneficiaries of trusts, between vendors and purchasers, lessors and lessees, mortgagors and mortgagees and employers and employees. As regards cohabitees, the position is rather uncertain. It is possible to insure the life of the other cohabitee to the extent of any joint indebtedness, for example where there is a mortgage. As most mortgages are protected by joint-life policies, such problems are unlikely to arise very much in practice. However, even where there is no mortgage, one cohabitee may wish to insure the life of the other, to be able to purchase the other's share of the house from his or her estate. This appears not to be possible. As yet, there is no case law on this point.

3.3 TYPES OF LIFE ASSURANCE POLICY

3.3.1 Endowment policies

The most common types of endowment policies currently available are the low-cost endowment policy, the with-profits policy and the without-profits policy. Each of these are dealt with below.

For income tax purposes, new policies will not qualify for tax relief on premiums. Policies taken out before 14 March 1984 may qualify for tax relief on the premiums and this is dealt with below. Most policies qualify for favourable income tax treatment on the policy proceeds. The life assurance company will always make clear to the policyholder whether or not the actual policy qualifies. Non-qualifying policies include single premium bonds and some unit-linked whole-life policies. Profits made on all non-qualifying life policies and, in certain limited circumstances, qualifying life policies are subject to higher rate income tax (Income and Corporation Taxes Act 1988, s 540). In these circumstances, profits for income tax purposes are assessed on regular premium policies by taking the proceeds and deducting the premiums paid. Profit on single premium policies is the excess of procceds over the premium. This sum is then 'top-sliced' (divided by the number of years the policy has been held) and the resulting figure added to the policyholder's income in the year of encashment. Particular care should be taken if a policy is being surrendered within 10 years of it being effected as it may lose its qualifying status.

Life Assurance Premium Relief (LAPR) is available on premiums paid to qualifying policies taken out before 14 March 1984, where the premiums are paid either by the policyholder or his spouse. The payer must also be a UK resident. The relief in the relevant section (ICTA 1988, s 266) is also available to 'any person who was that individual's spouse at the time the insurance or contract was made, unless the marriage was dissolved before 6 April 1979' (ICTA 1988, Sch 14, para 1). LAPR is given by the policyholder's withholding from the gross premium an amount equal to half the basic rate of tax. The total amount of gross premium eligible for relief is the higher of £1500 per tax year and one-sixth of the policyholder's total taxable income. If a pre-14 March 1984 policy is varied on or after that date so as to increase the policy benefits or extend the term of the insurance, LAPR will no longer be available. Variation will include the exercise of an option under convertible term policies, which are referred to below (see ICTA 1988, Sch 14, para 8 (3)–(5)). Special care should be taken when rewriting a joint life policy by removing the name of one policyholder to ensure that this does not constitute a 'variation' of the policy with the consequent loss of LAPR.

In this context, the family law practitioner should also consider the life assurance element that is available under personal pension schemes (ICTA 1988, s 637). Contributions under an approved personal pension policy are fully deductible from earnings for income tax purposes, and are, therefore, more advantageous than life policies, which attract LAPR. Life assurance may also be provided under the retirement annuity legislation (ICTA 1988, s 621(12)(b)), provided that the policy was effected before the 1 July 1988. Both types of policy can be assigned. Such policies are increasingly used as collateral security for borrowing purposes.

There is no charge to capital gains tax on the disposal of a policy, which includes payment of the sum assured or the payment of a sum on surrender of the policy, 'except where the person making the disposal is not the original beneficial owner and acquired the rights or interest for a consideration in money or money's worth' (Taxation of Chargeable Gains Act 1992, s 210). When considering an assignment from the original policyholder to a spouse or former spouse, this section should be borne in mind (see **6.3.1.2**(c)).

As to inheritance tax consequences, see **3.4**.

Quotations from insurance companies for both endowment and other policies will be similar, because the LAUTRO rules now govern the assumed growth rates upon which those quotations are based. Rates of seven per cent and 10.5 per cent per annum are used. These are not forecasts, however, and should only be used as general guides. It is important to consult a reputable and experienced broker on all aspects of investment, especially with regard to the performance of the different insurance companies.

3.3.1.1 Low-cost endowment policies

Low-cost endowment policies are a combination of an endowment with profits and decreasing term assurance (see **3.3.1.2** and **3.3.6**) and were developed in connection with mortgages. The purpose of them is to provide borrowers with a cheaper form of policy. Under these policies, the sum assured under the endowment element is less than the outstanding capital under the mortgage. In order to satisfy building societies that the mortgage will be repaid, calculations are based upon cautious assumptions as to future returns and profits. This explains why the sum assured in proposal forms is often far lower than might have been expected – sometimes alarmingly so in the context of the mortgage which is being arranged and the appropriate death benefit. However, the decreasing term assurance element provides repayment of any shortfall under the endowment policy, should death occur before the maturity date.

3.3.1.2 With-profits policies

With-profits policies are the traditional type of savings policy; premiums are usually paid monthly and invested in a policy that provides a basic life assurance sum which is the amount payable on death.

Each year, an actuarial valuation is carried out to determine the profits of the insurance company. Profits are then added to the sum assured so that the policy value gradually grows. There are two types of profits, reversionary bonuses and terminal bonuses. The former are added to the policy each year and cannot subsequently be removed: the latter are added to the policy only when a claim is made, whether on death or maturity. Terminal bonuses are more volatile since they depend upon how the particular company views the economic outlook at the time the bonus is assessed.

Typically, an endowment policy is used as collateral security for the mortgage of the matrimonial home. The benefit of the policy will be assigned to the mortgagee. During the term of the mortgage, interest only will be paid to the mortgagee while the premiums will be paid direct to the insurance company. On maturity, the benefit is then paid direct to the mortgagee to cover the redemption figure and the additional administrative costs. Any benefit remaining is payable to the beneficiary of the policy.

When a policy is surrendered, the policyholder does not receive the full value of all the profits that have been added to the policy. Early surrender or cancellation can lead to a poor return on the investment. It may be more advantageous to sell the policy; details of how such policies can be auctioned are given at **6.3.1.2**(e). Only as a last resort should such a policy be surrendered.

It is possible to leave the investment with its 'paid up' value, even when the policyholder cannot afford to carry on with the premiums. Instead of surrendering the policy, the policyholder keeps the accrued investment value and avoids the penalties against early surrender. The policy is effectively frozen for the rest of the term until the policy matures. At that point a reduced sum is paid but without the further penalties for early surrender.

3.3.1.3 Without-profits policies

Without-profits policies maintain the same amount of benefit throughout the term of the policy; the policyholder does not share in the profits of the insurance company. Although the premiums are much lower than those under with-profits policies, the value of the return may decline in real terms in line with inflation.

3.3.2 Unit-linked savings policies

Unit-linked savings policies used to be less common than endowment policies, probably because the amount of the benefit is related to the performance of the particular investment fund and the policyholder, who is likely to be apprehensive about the return on his or her premiums, carries that risk. On the other hand, these policies may provide a greater return than may be obtained through the traditional endowment policy. Building societies are generally happy to use these policies as collateral for mortgages. These policies also contain a life cover element, as would be the case with a with-profits policy.

The regular premiums buy units in whichever life assurance fund the particular company offers. There is usually a range of funds from which to choose: equities, fixed interest, international equities, property and so on. If the particular fund rises in value, then so will the value of the units held; but the reverse can also apply and the value may fall – something the family law practitioner should bear in mind particularly when trying to raise cash to meet specific needs or liabilities

The premiums buy units at the offer price; when the policy is encashed, those same units are sold at the bid price. The 'spread' between the bid and offer prices at any one time is usually around five per cent. This sum covers part of the life assurance administration charges; in addition, most funds will make a further management charge of 0.75 per cent per annum of the value of the overall fund. Similar administrative charges are incurred in the case of endowment policies, but with unit-linked policies these charges tend to be more easily ascertained.

3.3.3 Whole-life policies

As the name suggests, whole-life policies provide permanent life assurance protection. The sum assured will be payable only upon death, whenever that may occur, providing the contract is still in force. These policies, like endowment policies, can be either with or without profits.

Depending on the type of policy, the premium payable will usually stay at a level amount throughout the course of the policy, although these may be limited to a set age; for example, the premium may cease to be paid when the policyholder is 65, although the policy would continue in force. The policy commences with a guaranteed sum assured, which will never fall.

Each year, as happens for with-profits endowment policies, a decision is made about how much surplus is available. A bonus is declared which enhances the benefits payable. Once these bonuses are added, they cannot subsequently be removed or reduced. These reversionary bonuses form part of the guaranteed return at the time of a claim.

A further bonus is often added at the time of a claim (the terminal or claims bonus). This bonus usually represents surplus profits and reflects how well the fund has performed during the course of the contract.

Whole-life policies have a surrender value, so that after an initial period of approximately two years there would be a level of return should the policy be cancelled. However, the policy should not be looked upon as a form of investment, as its real purpose is to provide long-term life cover. In exceptional circumstances, it may be possible to sell a whole-life policy (see **6.3.1.2**(e)).

3.3.4 Level-term assurance

Level-term assurance policies are effected for a specific period or term. For the lump sum to be payable, death has to occur within the specified term. As with the other policies, premiums are payable throughout that term.

When considering methods of providing security for children's maintenance, for example by effecting a term policy until a child attains a specific age, the premiums payable under this type of policy will be very much lower than under an endowment policy or a whole-life policy.

Where such a policy is cancelled before the end of the term, there will be no surrender value.

3.3.5 Convertible-term assurance

Convertible-term assurance is a variation of the term assurance policy. It enables the policyholder to convert the policy at any time during the course of the contract to another form of assurance. It may be converted to a whole-life policy or to an endowment policy; it is important to note that such conversion can take place without any further evidence as to the life assured's health being provided. Thus, whatever the state of health of the life assured, no further medical evidence will be needed. Although the premiums themselves would increase by reason of the conversion, there will be no additional loading to the premiums.

Until conversion, the policy works as a straightforward term assurance policy, and so has no surrender value at that stage.

The benefits of this type of policy are clear, particularly on marriage breakdown. They provide a relatively cheap form of life assurance from the beginning, but the conversion options give considerable flexibility in the future.

3.3.6 Decreasing-term assurance

Decreasing-term assurance is another variant of the basic-term assurance policy. Mortgage protection policies are well-known examples of this type of policy. As the name suggests, the amount of cover reduces each year. They provide possibly the most economic way to provide cover for maintenance payments.

There is no surrender value in the case of this type of policy.

3.3.7 Joint-life policies

All the types of policy described above can be written on joint lives. Most joint-life policies are written so that the policy matures on the death of the first of the policyholders to die; 'last-survivor' policies are most frequently used in making provision for inheritance tax. The disadvantage of having a joint-life policy, as against two separate policies, is that the survivor will be left without any cover. Further, where, for example, both husband and wife are killed in a car crash, only one lump sum is payable: the relatively small increase in premiums needed to provide two policies may be better value and may be more effective in providing for children.

Life insurance companies will usually be quite flexible about rewriting the policy by removing the name of one policyholder from the policy. This is sometimes requested, particularly after divorce, in an effort to reduce the premiums. It is good practice to have a full deed of assignment (see Appendix, precedent 11) prepared in any event, otherwise it could be argued that the existing benefit still belongs to the original policyholder. Despite the prospect of a reduction in premiums, it may still be worthwhile to continue a policy on a joint-life basis. For example, where a wife is using the policy as security for a mortgage after divorce, it may still be desirable to retain the life assurance cover in the husband's name, particularly if he is paying maintenance to support the wife or a child who is living with her. Practitioners should be careful not to lose the tax relief on premiums which is available on policies taken out before 13 March 1984 (ICTA 1988, s 266(3)) (see **3.3.1**).

3.3.8 Other types of insurance

3.3.8.1 Family income benefit

Contracts for payment of family income benefit provide cover by supplying an income for a selected term of years. For example, the period chosen could be until children reach a particular age, or could end with the repayment of a loan or an obligation to pay school fees.

The policies provide for payment of a regular monthly sum from the time of the claim. The right to claim normally arises on the death of the policyholder.

This type of contract has no investment content whatsoever, and so nothing is payable at the end of the term. Nor is there any surrender value.

Effectively, the amount of cover is decreasing; for example, if the contract has only one year left to run when the claim is made, only one year's benefit would be payable. By contrast, with a term policy, the full lump-sum figure would still be paid out.

Benefits paid under this type of contract are not aggregated to other income for tax purposes. LAPR is available on pre-14 March 1984 policies (see **3.3.1**).

In practice, most companies will allow the benefit to be commuted for a lump sum, although the amount cannot be negotiated until the time of the claim.

3.3.8.2 Permanent health insurance

Permanent health insurance policies are intended to meet long-term disability. The benefit is normally payable after a period ('the deferred period') has elapsed from the onset of the disability; the minimum such period is 4 weeks and, more usually, benefit is payable after an even longer period, often between 13 and 26 weeks.

This type of policy should not be confused with personal accident and sickness arrangements, which normally pay a benefit after a period of absence from work through incapacity of around seven days, but only for a maximum of one or two years. Permanent health insurance is expensive, because the likelihood of a claim over the length of the term covered is much greater.

Most permanent health insurance policies pay a benefit, either monthly or weekly, to the policyholder, from the end of the deferred period until the policyholder returns to work or reaches 'the ceasing age' – his sixtieth birthday for example. The earlier the ceasing age, the lower the premium will be. The benefit can either be at a fixed rate or can be increased, usually by five per cent for each year after the claim has been made, but policies are available under which the increases are calculated from the beginning of the policy itself.

Some provide for the policyholder to receive a proportion of the benefit where he takes up another occupation at a lower salary because of the disability and there will sometimes be a rehabilitation benefit to enable the policyholder to return to his or her original occupation, but at a lower capacity.

Normally, the benefit is treated as investment income. However, under a special concession from the Inland Revenue, in the first complete tax year in which benefits are received, they are ignored for tax purposes (IR Extra Statutory Concession A26).

3.3.8.3 Divorce maintenance plan

It is possible to obtain specialised policies to protect maintenance payments. For example, the Consolidated Insurance Group has produced a policy which combines life cover for a fixed term with accident and sickness benefit.

On death, a lump sum is payable which is equivalent to the commuted value of the maintenance payments; if the payer of maintenance is unable to work or suffers a drop in his earnings because of an accident or sickness, maintenance will be paid for a maximum period of 12 months. Another feature of this policy is that the amounts payable may be increased to take account of any variation of maintenance that is agreed or ordered.

Despite the obvious attractions of a policy which is specifically designed to help those considering arrangements after marriage breakdown, it is well worth looking at the benefits on offer, which may not all be suitable for the needs of the particular family: other policies on the market may be more suitable and cost effective.

3.4 ASSIGNING THE BENEFIT OF A POLICY: CREATING TRUSTS OF POLICIES

Unless otherwise stated, the benefit of a policy will belong to the person who has taken the policy out – whether the proposer or the life assured. For example, if a man takes out a whole-life policy on his own life, with the intention of providing for his dependants, the sum assured will belong to him beneficially and will be paid into his estate. As such, inheritance tax will be payable on this sum. To avoid the sum assured falling into the estate and suffering inheritance tax, the policyholder must either have assigned the policy or have declared a trust of the beneficial interest in favour of, for example, his dependants. Consideration must still be given as to whether the assignment or the continued premium payments might constitute a gift, which would have inheritance tax consequences.

3.4.1 Assignments

Assignments are most frequently encountered as part of the arrangements for an endowment mortgage. In such cases, the benefit of the endowment policy is assigned to the mortgagee, who will reassign the policy if the mortgage is redeemed before the end of the term, for example on a sale of the property. It may also be necessary to assign policies on marriage breakdown, from one spouse to the other, or from the joint names of both parties into the sole name of one.

A draft deed of assignment is included in the Appendix, precedent 11.

3.4.1.1 Statutory assignment

The old common law rule was that no chose in action could be assigned without the assent of the debtor. However, the Policies of Assurance Act 1867 makes it possible to assign a life assurance policy without such assents. The effect of such an assignment is that the assignee can sue upon the policy in his own name.

Under the 1867 Act, three conditions have to be satisfied:

(a) the assignee must have a good title in equity (s 1);
(b) written notice must be given to the insurer (s 3); and
(c) a written instrument of assignment must be executed (s 5).

Subsequent legislation was passed to ensure that all 'legal things in action' could be legally assigned. Section 136 of the Law of Property Act 1925 (LPA 1925) requires that:

> 'absolute assignment by writing under the hand of the assignor (not purporting to be by way of charge only) of any debt or other legal thing in action, of which express notice in writing has been given to the debtor, trustee or other person from whom the assignor would have been entitled to claim such debt or thing in action.'

Since LPA 1925 specifically saves the earlier legislation, the relationship between the two pieces of legislation is less than clear. Most commentators recommend that LPA 1925 should be relied upon, since it does not require the assignee to prove that he has good title in equity as a condition precedent for the legal assignment.

For the assignment to take effect under LPA 1925, the following conditions must be satisfied:

(a) there must be an absolute assignment of the entire policy;
(b) the assignment must be in writing signed by the assignor, not necessarily by deed although that is generally preferred;
(c) express notice in writing must be given to the debtor – this is best done by sending a copy of the deed to the life assurance company.

3.4.1.2 Equitable assignment

If the statutory requirements are not satisfied, an assignment may nevertheless operate as an equitable assignment. The equitable assignment may later become a legal assignment, for example upon notice being given to the life assurance company. Equity also imposes conditions which must be satisfied if an assignment is to be given any effect. For example, there must be some transaction which shows that there is an existing intention to assign. Further, there must be some action on the part of the assignor as part of the assignment; for example, in *Thomas v Harris* [1947] 1 All ER 444, a man handed some insurance policies on his life to his son and requested that a tombstone be erected for him out of the policy monies; this was held to constitute a valid equitable assignment.

3.4.1.3 Assignment to two or more persons

If the assignment is to two or more persons, they may take as joint tenants or as tenants in common. It seems that a tenancy in common of a chose in action is possible in equity, but not at law. Joint tenants may sever their joint tenancy by a simple notice of severance.

3.4.2 Trusts of life assurance policies

There are three ways of establishing a trust, so that the benefit of a life assurance policy passes to somebody other than the assured:

(a) through the Married Woman's Property Act 1882, s 11, to a spouse or child;
(b) through an express declaration of trust by the assured in favour of persons other than his or her spouse or children; and
(c) by an assignment of the policy to trustees who will then hold the policy for the named beneficiaries.

3.4.2.1 Trusts under the Married Woman's Property Act 1882

The simplest way of declaring a trust to one's spouse or children is through the Married Woman's Property Act 1882 (MWPA 1882), s 11.

> 'A policy of assurance effected by any man on his own life, and expressed to be for the benefit of his wife, or of his children, or of his wife and children, or any of them, or by any woman on her own life, and expressed to be for the benefit of her husband, or of her children, or of her husband and children, or any of them, shall create a trust in favour of the objects therein named, and the monies payable under any such policy shall not, so long as any object of the trust remains unperformed, form part of the estate of the insured, or be subject to his or her debts.'

The insured may, by any memorandum, appoint a trustee or trustees of the monies payable under the policy. If no trustee is appointed, then the policy will vest in the insured and his or her legal personal representatives, who will then hold the monies as trustees. It should be noted that s 11 does not provide a power to appoint.

Most insurance companies have their own standard form of memorandum, which provides the trustees with wider powers of investment than those given under the Trustee Investment Act 1961. Practitioners should check whether there is a charging clause in the memorandum, particularly if they are appointed as trustees.

For the purposes of the MWPA 1882, 'children' includes illegitimate or adopted children, but not grandchildren or stepchildren.

3.4.2.2 Naming the beneficiary

If the policy names a beneficiary, then that beneficiary acquires an immediate vested interest. Otherwise, for example, if the policy appoints 'my wife', then the wife will take only a contingent interest; if she fits the description on the death of the assured, the contingent interest will vest in her.

In the case of *Re Browne's Policy* [1903] 1 Ch 188, the assured had stated that the policy was 'for the benefit of his wife and children'. The wife, living at the date of the policy, had predeceased the policy owner, who was survived by his second wife and the children of both marriages. It was held that the second wife and all the children, of both marriages, should take the benefit of the policy as joint tenants. It is helpful to contrast this with the case of *Cousins v Sun Life Assurance Society* [1933] Ch 126, where the policyholder stated that the policy should be 'for the benefit of Lilian Cousins, the wife of the life assured'. Although the wife predeceased the policyholder, in this case it was held that the wife took an immediate absolute vested interest in the property, which passed on her death to her personal representatives. In practice, such questions of interpretation will rarely arise because of the specific powers of appointment under a memorandum or express deed of trust. The family law practitioner should ask for details of any memorandum or trust provision on disclosure, as well as the surrender values and anticipated maturity benefits of the policies.

Divorce will not of itself destroy the interest of a wife named as a beneficiary under a trust. It should be borne in mind that the court, under MCA 1973, s 24(1)(c), is able to vary the terms of any such trust. It is important, therefore, to ensure that details of such trusts are considered, and included in the terms of any order made.

3.4.2.3 Assignment to trustees

In view of the amounts which are involved, it is good practice to assign the benefit of a policy to trustees where there are no proper trust provisions in existence, particularly where children are intended to benefit. The trust document can then set out in full the wider powers of investment, the power to appoint new trustees and so on. A simple form of trust may be suitable where a policy is intended to provide security for children's maintenance. More flexible trust arrangements giving the trustees additional powers, or even a full discretionary trust, may be preferred. The effect of inheritance tax should also be considered carefully in this context.

3.5 LIFE ASSURANCE AND THE LOW INCOME FAMILY

In calculating income support, the surrender value of any life assurance policy will be disregarded (Income Support (General) Regulations 1987, SI 1987/1967, as amended, reg 46(2) and Sch 10).

For the purposes of income support, housing costs do not include premiums under life assurance policies, even where the policy is used as collateral security for the mortgage.

CHAPTER 4

LEGAL FRAMEWORK: STATUTE AND CASE-LAW

4.1 INTRODUCTION

A husband may, for many years, have made contributions into a pension fund, planning with his wife towards a financially secure retirement. The family will often have made financial sacrifices so that the contributions can be made.

Divorce will not only deprive the wife of the prospect of sharing in her husband's pension and any lump sum payable under the scheme upon retirement but also deprive her of the security of any widow's benefit that may have been payable had the marriage continued and her husband predeceased her.

The court does not have specific power to deal with contingent pension benefits and, although it does have wide powers under the Matrimonial Causes Act 1973 to deal with the division of assets on divorce, there are still cases where the making of appropriate provision for the wife, which may for example be insurance-based, does not fall within the power of the court. There may be insufficient assets immediately available to compensate the wife for the loss of future benefits and she may, in any event, find herself faced with an argument that resources which might provide a fund sufficient to satisfy her claims will not become available in the foreseeable future and are not, therefore, resources to which the court must have regard.

There may be alternatives open to the wife, such as seeking a larger share of those assets which are immediately available, or delaying the making, or seeking an adjournment, of her application for a lump sum order, but these may also be unsatisfactory in the particular circumstances of the case. Further, the statutory defences designed to protect the blameless wife from being divorced against her will, with the resulting loss of pension benefits, will not be available to her, unless the divorce proceedings are based on specified facts.

In this chapter we will explore how statute and case-law may help or hinder a wife in her search for financial security in her later years when she is faced with divorce proceedings.

4.2 THE MATRIMONIAL CAUSES ACT 1973

The court has wide powers to make financial provision and/or property adjustment under the Matrimonial Causes Act 1973 ('the 1973 Act'), as amended by the Matrimonial and Family Proceedings Act 1984 ('the 1984 Act'), on granting a decree of divorce, nullity of marriage or judicial separation, or at any time thereafter.

When considering how best to exercise its powers under the 1973 Act, the court must have regard to the matters set out in s 25. Of particular relevance when considering the loss of pension benefits are the factors set out in s 25(2)(a) and s 25(2)(h) of the 1973 Act. Under s 25(2)(a), the court must have regard to 'the income, earning capacity, property and other financial resources which each of the parties to the marriage has or is likely to have in *the foreseeable future* [sic] . . .' and under s 25(2)(h) 'in the case of proceedings for divorce or nullity of marriage, the value to each of the parties to the marriage of any benefit *for example, a pension* [sic] which, by reason of the dissolution or annulment of the marriage, that party will lose the chance of acquiring'.

Prior to the 1984 Act, the courts were also obliged to exercise their powers so as to place the parties, so far as was practicable and having regard to their conduct, in the financial position in which they would have been if the marriage had not broken down and each had properly discharged his or her financial obligations and responsibilities towards the other. That obligation, which strengthened the position of a wife who stood to lose the enjoyment of future funds or widow's benefits under a pension scheme, was removed by the 1984 Act.

The 1984 Act did not, however, change the range of orders that the court could make, and the opportunity was not taken to include a specific power for the court to deal with contingent pension benefits.

4.3 THE FORESEEABLE FUTURE

The income and any lump sum payable under a pension scheme are financial resources. If, however, they are not payable within the foreseeable future, they are not resources to which the court must have regard under s 25(2)(a) of the 1973 Act. Hence, they may have little relevance except as a piece of background to the case (*Hedges v Hedges* [1991] 1 WLR 196). Even if there are no other assets immediately available against which the wife could pursue an application for a lump sum order, if anticipated resources are not payable within the foreseeable future, her application for a lump sum order may well be dismissed (*Michael v Michael* [1986] 2 FLR 389, CA). So, in what circumstances are such resources payable in the foreseeable future and, hence, relevant under s 25(2)(a) of the 1973 Act?

In *Richardson v Richardson* (1978) Fam Law 86, the Court of Appeal considered three years hence to be the foreseeable future. The husband, a senior civil servant, was entitled to retire in three years, when he would receive a lump sum of £9000. Additionally, had the wife survived the husband and had the marriage continued, she would have been entitled to a widow's pension.

The judge awarded the wife a lump sum of £7750. The wife appealed, contending that the judge should have taken into account, inter alia, the loss of pension rights and should further have had regard to the husband's lump sum payable on retirement. Ormrod LJ said that had the marriage subsisted, the wife would, together with the husband, have had the benefit of the lump sum. Equally, some attention should be paid to the wife's loss of pension rights, and regard should be had to the lump sum payment which the husband would receive. The order made at first instance was, he said, insufficient. The Court of Appeal increased the lump sum to £12,000.

In *Richardson*, the court was able to compensate the wife for lost benefits by increasing her share of the existing assets. Such assets may not always be available and the wife may have no alternative but to seek either an immediate order for the payment of a lump sum in the future, when there are further assets available for distribution, or an order for a lump sum payable by instalments, where the second or subsequent instalments fall due when the anticipated resource has been received. Alternatively, she may seek an adjournment of her application for a lump sum order (see **4.4**) or delay the making of her application until there are funds available against which she can endeavour to pursue her claims (see **4.5**).

In *Priest v Priest* (1980) FLR 189, the Court of Appeal considered that a lump sum payable in five years was sufficiently proximate to be regarded as the foreseeable future. The husband was a Royal Marine and, if he completed a minimum of 22 years' service, he would receive a gratuity. When the parties separated in 1976, his expectation was that in 1983 he would receive £3975. By June of 1978, when the wife's application for ancillary relief was considered, that expectation had increased to £5229, and he could have continued to serve until 1993, by which time his gratuity would be significantly larger.

On the wife's appeal, Cumming-Bruce LJ held that an expectation of a gratuity was a financial resource which the husband was likely to have in the future; the husband was likely to have a financial resource of £5229 in 1983, five years hence, and this he regarded as sufficiently proximate to be regarded as in the foreseeable future. The husband was ordered to pay the wife one-third of £5229, if and when he received his gratuity, even though that might not be until 1993.

An order of this nature, providing for the payment of a fraction of the gratuity to be paid to the wife when received, could not at that time, and cannot now, be made against the gratuity of a soldier or airman, by virtue of s 203 of the Army Act 1955 and s 203 of the Air Force Act 1955 (see **4.8**). For some years, there was doubt about the powers of the court in relation to the making of a lump sum order against Naval and Royal Marine gratuities. That doubt has, in relation to these two services, now been removed by the Armed Forces Act 1991, which prevents the court from making an order such as that made in *Priest*. It is worthy of note that although the sum the husband in *Priest* stood to receive was likely to have increased by the time he received it, even if that were in 1983, the Court of Appeal specified the capital sum of which the wife was to have one-third, namely the £5229 which the husband was likely to have in 1983, unlike *Milne v Milne* (1981) FLR 286, CA. In *Milne*, the court was prepared to take into account, and make an order in respect of, a lump sum of £16,000, payable under a pension scheme ten years hence. The court ordered that, providing the wife was surviving at the material time, the husband should pay one half of the amount to which he or his estate should become entitled under the scheme.

In the later case of *Roberts v Roberts* [1986] 2 All ER 483, the court did not consider an Army gratuity, which would not be payable for at least six years, to be funds which were foreseeably available. On appeal, the court, in any event, held that the lump sum order amounted to a charge on that gratuity and was void under s 203 of the Army Act 1955, which is considered fully below (see **4.8**).

The authorities relating to foreseeable future assets were considered by Bracewell J in *MT v MT (Financial Provision: Lump Sum)* [1992] 1 FLR 362, when the wife requested an adjournment of her application for a lump sum order. There were no assets immediately available against which she could pursue her application but the husband would inherit assets on the death of his 83-year-old father. The wife succeeded in persuading the court that her application should be adjourned, even though the court did not know when the father would die and when the husband would therefore inherit; that he would receive monies on the death of his father was certain because of the operation of the law of Germany where the father was domiciled. It was held that as the father was likely to die within the next few years, his death was not a long-term matter, but foreseeable.

Hence, the foreseeable future has been held to extend for as much as 10 years as in *Milne*, although it is also worthy of note that the resource in that case was going to vest on a certain future date.

Although in *Roberts* the court did not consider that resources payable more than six years hence were foreseeably available, *Roberts* was decided by Wood J on a narrow point of breach of s 203 of the Army Act 1955, and therefore any other comment is obiter. The wife was not represented at the hearing and the case did not go to the Court of Appeal.

The case of *Hardy (see* **4.4.2**) was not referred to in *Roberts*.

4.4 ADJOURNMENT

Having established that a pension is a resource which is likely to be available 'in the foreseeable future', the orders which the court can make under the 1973 Act are limited to those contained in ss 23 and 24. There will, consequently, be cases where the law cannot adequately provide on an immediate basis for the loss of the chance of acquiring rights under a pension scheme. For example, the assets available for immediate distribution may be inadequate to compensate the wife for the benefits that she will lose on divorce, and yet her immediate needs, such as her need for a house, may dictate that she must pursue her claim for a lump sum order at once. *Bolsom v Bolsom* (1983) FLR 21 (see, however, *Barry v Barry* [1992] 2 WLR 799), makes it clear that a lump sum order is a once-and-for-all order and cannot take the form of an initial instalment to which the court can subsequently add further sums. The court cannot vary a lump sum order once made; and so, however far short of full compensation a lump sum payable under an order falls, the wife will not be able to seek an increase in the sum, or a second lump sum, when the husband subsequently receives the monies payable under his pension arrangements.

The court is not, of course, prevented from making a lump sum order payable by quantified or quantifiable instalments. Where there are some assets available immediately and others which are anticipated in the foreseeable future, such an order may provide a solution.

But what if there are simply no assets available for immediate distribution and the husband's income is such that he cannot pay sufficient maintenance to the wife so that she could make her own alternative pension arrangements, nor can he afford to replace the lost benefits by other means, such as taking out an insurance policy, a course of action which the court cannot, in any event, force him to follow (*Milne v Milne* (1981) FLR 286, CA)?

Faced with such difficulties, a wife can ask the court to adjourn her application for a lump sum order until such time as the anticipated resources are received, although whether or not the court will do so will depend on when it is anticipated that the monies will be received.

4.4.1 Adjourn – but for how long?

The court has not been prepared to adjourn such applications for as long as 10 years (*Milne v Milne* (1981) FLR 286), but has been prepared to grant adjournments for up to three years (*Morris v Morris* (1977) Fam Law 244, CA and *Davies v Davies* [1986] 1 FLR 497) and has indicated that a period of up to five years would be acceptable (*Roberts v Roberts* [1986] 2 FLR 152). Seven years was considered too long to grant an adjournment (*Ranson v Ranson* [1988] 1 FLR 292).

If the court decides that the future resource which the wife seeks to attack is not a resource that the husband will have in the foreseeable future, the wife's application for a lump sum order may well be dismissed rather than adjourned (*Michael v Michael* [1986] 2 FLR 389, CA).

These authorities were considered by Bracewell J in *MT v MT (Financial Provision: Lump Sum)* [1992] 1 FLR 362. Whilst not a pensions case, the court held that it had discretionary power to grant an adjournment of a wife's application for a lump sum where there were no assets against which the wife could pursue her claims, but justice between the parties demanded such an adjournment in the unusual circumstances of the case and there was a real possibility of capital from a specific source becoming available in the near future, upon the death of the husband's father. The only possibility of a clean break, which was desirable, was by an adjournment. The husband's father was aged 83 and was, in the court's view, likely to die within the next few years. The father's death was not, the court held, a long-term matter, but foreseeable.

In *Morris v Morris* (1977) Fam Law 244, the husband was a warrant officer in the Army who would receive a gratuity upon retirement. At first instance, the court ordered the husband to pay the wife one-quarter of the gratuity upon receipt and he appealed. The Court of Appeal did not consider s 203 of the Army Act 1955, which would have rendered void such an order (see **4.8**), but it did consider that it was neither practical, nor just, to make an immediate order for the payment of a lump sum or an immediate order for the payment in the future of a fraction of the lump sum and that the best course of action would be to stand over the wife's application for a lump sum with liberty to either party to restore.

The report of *Morris* does not give full details of the timing of the anticipated payment but these were obtained and set out by Ackner LJ in the later case of *Davies v Davies* (below) and it appears that the husband in *Morris* would become entitled to a gratuity two to three years hence, if he left the forces then.

In *Davies v Davies* [1986] 1 FLR 497, the court was again prepared to sanction an adjournment for two or three years, at which stage it was anticipated that assets would become available against which the wife could pursue her claims. It was, however, made clear that if there was no particular fund of money which a husband could anticipate receiving, the court should not order an adjournment merely because the future *might*, in some way or another, throw up a possible fund of capital against which the wife could pursue an application.

In *Davies*, the registrar made an order in a wife's favour for the payment of a lump sum, on the basis that the husband's farming partnership was failing and likely to be dissolved, thereby releasing capital. The husband appealed. The judge found that there was a real possibility that the dissolution of the partnership could occur in the foreseeable future but did not accept that the partnership was doomed. The judge decided that there was no valid basis for making an immediate lump sum order which would force the husband out of business. He adjourned generally the wife's application for a lump sum, with liberty to the parties to apply. The husband exercised his liberty to apply and then appealed to the Court of Appeal. He contended that the judge, having found that the application for an immediate lump sum was not sustainable, should have dismissed the application once and for all. Whilst supporting the principle that lump sum applications should ordinarily be disposed of once and for all, the Court of Appeal took the view that there was capital which was likely to become available for consideration in two or three years and the judge was, therefore, fully entitled to grant an adjournment.

At p 501, Ackner LJ held:

> 'It seems to me that the judge in that sort of situation was perfectly entitled, having resolved that there was no valid basis for an immediate order for a lump sum payment, to adjourn the application in order to see whether the event that he thought might well occur fairly soon, did in fact occur. That is not the same position as if the judge, anxious to preserve the wife's entitlement, should order an adjournment merely because the future might in some way or another throw up a

possible fund of capital, in regard to which the wife could make an application . . .'

The courts have indicated that the longest period that a matter should be adjourned is four to five years. This was the view expressed by Wood J in *Roberts v Roberts* [1986] 2 FLR 152. The husband was a serving soldier who would not receive a gratuity upon his discharge from the forces until April 1988. The parties had divided the family's existing capital and a consent order had been made for maintenance for the wife and children. There were no remaining capital resources besides the husband's gratuity. The matter came before the registrar in 1982, at which stage the earliest that the husband could receive his gratuity would be six years hence, in 1988.

The registrar made a lump sum order in the wife's favour and the husband, who was subsequently promoted to warrant officer, and would probably remain in the Army until the year 2003, sought and obtained leave to appeal out of time.

On appeal, the court found that, in any event, the order would be a charge on the husband's gratuity and clearly in breach of s 203 of the Army Act 1955 and, therefore, void (see **4.8**). The court further took the view that the wife's application should not be adjourned until the husband received his gratuity, as this might not be until 2003.

Referring to *Milne*, Wood J held, at p 156:

> 'that judgment indicates that it is undesirable to adjourn cases to an uncertain future and the longest period that the Court of Appeal seems to have in mind about those decisions is some four to five years and that, in my judgment, is about the longest period that would be appropriate.'

4.4.2 A longer adjournment?

In *Milne v Milne* (1981) FLR 286, the court was not prepared to adjourn the wife's application for a lump sum order for a period of 10 years, at which time it was anticipated that the husband would receive the lump sum payable under his pension scheme.

In refusing to grant the wife the adjournment suggested, Purchas J commented, at p 286:

> 'For my part, I have come to the conclusion that that would not be the right approach. I have in mind the general concept of the 1973 Act, as referred to by Lord Scarman in *Minton v Minton* [1979] AC 593, that, if possible, the parties should know and come to some situation where they can look forward rather than back. If an adjournment were granted neither of the parties would really know where they stood and that would not be advantageous to either.'

The Court of Appeal was prepared to grant an indefinite adjournment in the non-pension case of *Hardy v Hardy* (1981) FLR 321, where the husband's family was very wealthy and, although the husband had no assets, there was a very real expectation that he would become a wealthy man at some stage in the future. However, Ormrod LJ commented at p 323 that this was a very unusual case on its facts and it may not be a useful precedent.

4.5 DELAYING THE APPLICATION

An alternative to the filing and subsequent adjournment of an application for a lump sum is to delay the making of the application until a time in the future when the anticipated resource has become available for distribution.

By s 23(1) of the 1973 Act, the court, on an application, might make a lump sum order on granting a decree or any time thereafter. There is no statute or rule limiting the time, but if a wife remarries before making her application she may not subsequently apply for financial provision (s 28(3) of the 1973 Act). However, provided she has not remarried when the application is made, a wife may still obtain an order for a lump sum or property adjustment, even if she has remarried by the time the application is heard. It is the prayer in the petition or answer, and not the notice of intention to proceed, which constitutes the application (*Jackson v Jackson* [1973] 2 All ER 395). Care must therefore be taken to include the appropriate prayer in the pleadings.

That the court has jurisdiction to hear an application for a lump sum order, even when a considerable period of time has passed since the pronouncement of the decree nisi, was confirmed in *Twiname v Twiname* [1992] 1 FLR 29. Although, in that case, the wife's petition included a prayer for all forms of ancillary relief, the only order made at the time of the divorce was for periodical payments. Some 15 years after the pronouncement of the decree nisi, the husband sold his business for £6,000,000 and the wife made a further application seeking a lump sum. The husband argued that the wife was not entitled to apply for a lump sum after such an extensive period of delay, but the Court of Appeal agreed with the decision of the registrar and the judge on subsequent appeal, namely, that the court was not prevented from dealing with the wife's application for a lump sum order despite the passing of time.

Whether or not the court, on considering the application, would find it appropriate to make a lump sum order in favour of the wife is, however, another matter. A wife making such a delayed application may find herself faced with the argument that after a lapse of time it would be unjust to award a lump sum out of assets in the accrual or acquisition of which the wife had played no part.

Attention was drawn to this argument in the case of *Pearce v Pearce* (1980) FLR 261, where at the time of the divorce in 1969 the wife made no application for a lump sum payment as the husband was then an undischarged bankrupt. In 1978, the husband's father transferred to him a half share of a house. Six months later, following the father's death, his half share in the house passed to the husband together with a substantial lump sum of money. The wife applied for a lump sum order and succeeded. On the husband's appeal, the judge confirmed the order. The husband appealed to the Court of Appeal contending that the judge had erred in:

(a) awarding the wife any lump sum at all in view of the time that had elapsed from the dissolution of the marriage; and

(b) awarding the wife a lump sum from capital resources of the husband not generated in the course of the marriage but acquired by gift and inheritance some nine years after the dissolution of the marriage.

At p 264, Ormrod LJ, whilst not accepting the first gound of appeal, nevertheless held:

> 'That does not mean to say, however, that the court should give any encouragement to persons, wives or husbands, to make application for lump sum or property adjustment orders long after the divorce has taken place. At the same time it makes it clear that the court retains its jurisdiction to entertain such applications in cases where the circumstances are unusual or where there are good reasons for thinking that the justice of the case requires the court to make a lump sum order, even though a long period of time has elapsed since the marriage was dissolved. In other words, lapse of time is an important factor to be taken into account in the exercise of discretion under s 25 of the 1973 Act. It is part of "all the circumstances of the case", and in some cases it will be a very important circumstance: it may be a decisive circumstance but in this case the facts are so extreme'.

The husband had never paid any maintenance for his former wife or children and the wife had relied solely upon social security. The court felt that those circumstances went a long way to eliminating the lapse of time argument.

In *Hardy v Hardy* (1981) FLR 321, the court reiterated the principle that the wife did not have to make her application for a lump sum order in 1981 when the husband had no assets, and that it was reasonable, sensible and proper for her to limit any claim to periodical payments. If a long period elapsed before the wife made her claim for a lump sum, the court would take account of any factors arising from that lapse of time, such as an improvement in the husband's finances.

One would hope, however, that where there was a capital resource such as a pension, the right to which accrued, albeit partly, during the years of the marriage (although the benefit would be received at some time in the future), the lapse of time argument would have less strength than in a case where the husband's wealth was not earned during the marriage but acquired afterwards.

Nevertheless, since such exceptional circumstances as prevailed in the *Pearce* case may not often arise, a decision to delay the making of an application should be taken carefully. However, if there are simply no assets available against which the wife can pursue an immediate claim and if an adjournment of the application is inappropriate, she will have nothing to lose by delaying her application. When making the decision to delay the making of the application, it may well be appropriate to indicate to the husband's solicitors that an application will be pursued at a later stage. If a 'lapse of time' argument is raised when the application is later pursued, it can at least be met with the reply that the husband has not been taken by surprise by the application.

A wife who has chosen to delay the making of her application for a lump sum may, when later pursuing the application, find herself faced not only with the lapse of time argument but also with an argument that the court should not award her a lump sum from capital resources which were not generated in the course of the marriage but acquired, for example, by gift and inheritance after the dissolution of the marriage. This argument formed the basis of the husband's second ground of appeal in *Pearce*.

The court held in *Pearce* that the word 'resources' in s 25 of the 1973 Act is entirely unqualified, and there are no words of limitation upon it. Hence, the fact that the resources were acquired after the divorce did not mean that they were resources which the court should exclude, although the fact that they were so acquired was a relevant consideration.

In *Schuller v Schuller* [1990] 2 FLR 193, Butler-Sloss LJ considered the argument that after-acquired assets which the wife had inherited after the parties separated should be treated in a different way from money which had been acquired during the continuance of cohabitation. She held, following *Pearce*, that the wife's after-acquired assets were extremely relevant in deciding what capital provision she was entitled to from the capital assets of the marriage and were properly taken into account in the court below.

4.6 THE STATUTORY DEFENCES

In cases where the limits upon the court's powers or the absence of adequate income and/or capital prevent the court from making an order that will fully compensate the wife for the pension benefits lost on divorce, how can a wife invoke statute to protect herself?

This is of particular concern in cases where a blameless wife finds herself faced with divorce proceedings issued, against her will, on the fact of five years' separation. The 1973 Act provides protection in the form of two different defences, namely under s 5 and s 10.

4.6.1 Grave financial hardship – section 5 of the Matrimonial Causes Act 1973

4.6.1.1 The statutory provision

Section 5 of MCA 1973 enables a respondent to a divorce petition, based on five years' separation, to oppose the grant of a decree on the ground that the dissolution of the marriage will result in grave financial or other hardship and that it would, in all the circumstances, be wrong to dissolve the marriage. Where the grant of a decree is opposed under this section, then, if the court finds that the petitioner is entitled to rely on five years' separation and makes no finding as to any other fact and, if apart from s 5 the court would grant a decree of divorce, the court must consider all the circumstances, including the conduct of the parties, the interests of the parties and any children or other persons concerned and, if it is of the opinion that the dissolution of the marriage will result in grave financial or other hardship and in all the circumstances it would be wrong to dissolve the marriage, the petition must be dismissed.

Section 5(3) specifically provides that, for the purposes of the section, hardship includes the loss of the chance of acquiring any benefit which the respondent might acquire if the marriage were not dissolved. The hardship must result from the dissolution of the marriage and not from the breakdown (*Talbot v Talbot* (1971) 115 Sol Jo 870).

The meaning of grave financial hardship was considered by Dunn J in *Talbot*, when he held that grave financial hardship meant exactly what the words said and had to be considered subjectively in relation to the particular marriage and the circumstances in which the parties lived while it subsisted.

Grave does not mean no greater than de minimis, ie wholly trivial or of no practical significance. It has its ordinary meaning and 'if it were necessary . . . to use other words to provide guidance as to its meaning I would offer the words "important" or "very serious"' (per Megaw LJ in *Reiterbund v Reiterbund* [1975] 1 All ER 280 at p 285).

There are two obstacles that a respondent seeking to use this defence must overcome. The first is that she must show that she will suffer grave financial hardship as a result of the dissolution of the marriage and the second is that she must show that it would, in all the circumstances, be wrong to dissolve the marriage.

Dunn J held in *Talbot* (above) that in construing 'wrong' one had to have regard to all the circumstances of the persons involved, including the children, and to the balance which had to be maintained between upholding the sanctity of marriage and the desirability of ending empty ties.

Section 5 has limitations. It applies only when divorce proceedings have been issued on the basis of five years' separation. An adulterous wife who stands to lose considerable widow's benefit under her husband's pension arrangements could not block the decree absolute on a petition based on her adultery, under this section. Further, a wife must show not that she will lose something by being divorced but that she will suffer grave financial hardship (*Le Marchant v Le Marchant* [1977] 1 WLR 559 at p 562).

Section 5(2)(a) does not, as might be thought on first reading, prevent a respondent from seeking protection under this section if the petitioner could have taken proceedings on the basis of any other fact mentioned in s 1(2) of the 1973 Act, but had chosen, instead, to proceed on the basis of five years' separation. It means that the court must be satisfied only that the fact of five years' separation has been pleaded and proved, and no other fact has been pleaded and proved (*Rule v Rule* [1971] 3 All ER 1368).

4.6.1.2 The case-law

(a) The longer marriage and older spouse

Opposition to the granting of a decree under s 5 is more likely to succeed in a case involving a longer marriage and an older spouse, unless the husband is able to make appropriate provision compensating the wife for the loss she will suffer as a result of the divorce.

In the case of *Parker v Parker* [1972] 1 All ER 410, the parties were married in 1949, when the husband was 22 and the wife was 24, and separated in 1964. The case came before the court in 1972, when the wife was aged 47. The husband petitioned for divorce, relying on the fact that the parties had lived apart for a continuous period of at least five years, in accordance with s 2(1)(e) of the Divorce Reform Act 1969. The wife opposed the dissolution of the marriage under s 4(1) of that Act, which, in all material respects, was identical in its wording to s 5 of the 1973 Act. The wife argued that the financial benefits which she would or may lose on divorce were:

(i) loss of widow's State pension after the petitioner's death;
(ii) loss of police widow's pension after the petitioner's death;
(iii) as a single woman, increased national insurance contributions would be payable by her.

The loss of entitlement to the police widow's pension was considered by the court to be much the most important element of contingent loss. The possible loss ranged from £186, which would be payable if the petitioner died in police service on his salary current at that time, to £425, the maximum pension if the petitioner served for 30 years. The wife succeeded in persuading the court that she would suffer grave financial hardship if the marriage were dissolved, even though the loss of the police widow's pension was contingent upon her surviving her husband and the contingency was remote in time. However, the court was satisfied that the contingent loss of benefit from the police widow's pension could be offset out of the petitioner's financial resources by the purchase of a deferred annuity or a policy producing a specified minimum sum on maturity. The court did not consider that it was necessary, at that stage of the proceedings, to determine how this should be done or whether it should be done, and decided it was enough that resources were available which would enable compensation for the contingent loss to be achieved so that dissolution of itself would not result in grave financial hardship to the widow. On that basis the decree nisi was granted.

The defence succeeded in *Julian v Julian* (1972) 116 Sol Jo 763. This involved a long marriage where the parties were married in 1939 and, at the time of the hearing, the wife was aged 58. Although the husband had proposed that he would purchase an annuity which would provide the wife with £215 per annum, there was still a very substantial monetary gap between the financial provision the husband could make for the wife and the police widow's pension of £790 per annum, which she would have received if the marriage remained in existence and the husband predeceased her. The petition was therefore dismissed.

Parker was followed in *Le Marchant v Le Marchant* [1977] 1 WLR 559, although the court went further in protecting the wife when it required the husband to implement an offer put forward before the decree nisi could be made absolute. The wife opposed the dissolution of the marriage, contending that the loss of her index-linked widow's pension under the Post Office pension scheme would cause her grave financial hardship. The judge held that ss 5 and 10 of the 1973 Act had to be read together and that, since it was clear that the husband had the means to alleviate the financial hardship if appropriate orders were made under ss 10, 23 and 24 of the 1973 Act, the husband was entitled to a decree nisi. On appeal by the wife, it was held that the loss of an index-linked pension was evidence of grave financial hardship within the meaning of s 5(1) and, unless a petitioner could put forward a reasonably acceptable proposal sufficient to remove the element of grave financial hardship, the correct course was for the court to dismiss the petition. Although the husband's financial position enabled him to alleviate the wife's hardship if she had applied after decree nisi under s 10, this was not an adequate protection for the wife and, therefore, the petition should have been dismissed (or adjourned) to enable the husband to make a suitable offer. However, the husband had since put forward an acceptable proposal and the decree nisi should be allowed to stand on the terms that it would not be made absolute until the offer had been implemented.

Of concern, however, are the comments made by Ormrod LJ in *Le Marchant* at p 562 where he held:

> 'It would be quite wrong to approach this kind of case on the footing that the wife is entitled to be compensated pound for pound for what she will lose in consequence of the divorce. She has to show not that she will lose something by being divorced, but that she will suffer grave financial hardship which is quite another matter altogether.'

It should be noted that this comment was made in the context of a defence to divorce and not in relation to an ancillary relief application.

The onus of proving grave financial hardship lies on the wife seeking to invoke the protection offered under s 5 of the 1973 Act. Ormrod LJ in *Le Marchant* gives helpful guidance on the procedure to be followed. He supports the comments made by Cumming-Bruce J in *Parker*, confirming that the right approach in these cases is that the pleadings should allege by way of answer the grave financial hardship relied upon. The petitioner's reply should meet that allegation, if it is possible to meet it, with sufficient detail. Discovery can then be sought and obtained in the ordinary way so that the court has available the relevant financial information which it will require when considering the wife's position.

The defence also succeeded in the case of *Lee v Lee* (1973) 117 Sol Jo 616, again a case involving an older wife, who was aged 62. Although the husband's financial proposals to the wife, including his proposals to compensate her for the loss of civil servant's widow pension, were considered by the court to be not ungenerous, the provision proffered was not sufficient for the wife to buy a one-roomed flat in the area of her son's home where her son was seriously ill and required his mother to look after him.

(b) The shorter marriage – the younger wife

The court has been less inclined to allow protection to the younger wife in a shorter marriage. The defence failed in the case of *Mathias v Mathias* [1972] 3 WLR 201. The parties married in 1962, when the wife was aged 22 and the husband aged 25. The parties separated in 1964. When the matter came before the court in 1972, the wife was aged 32. The wife opposed the decree on the husband's petition based on five years' separation, arguing that she would lose an army widow's pension and a State widow's pension if the marriage were dissolved. She also argued that there would be financial loss to the child of the marriage if the marriage were dissolved and the husband remarried, because the husband's father's will provided that on the death of the husband's mother his children should share in equal shares. The wife's concern was that her husband's remarriage may mean the birth of another child who would benefit under the will, thus depriving her own child. Karminski LJ distinguished this case from *Parker*, commenting:

> 'An important fact in that case was that the wife there was a good deal older than the wife in this case and the financial hardship there related not to a lady in the early thirties but to a lady in the late forties. Those are material matters in considering the gravity, if any, of the financial hardship.'

The court accepted that the wife was bound to suffer some degree of financial hardship but that in the circumstances generally it would not, in any event, be wrong to dissolve the marriage.

Dicta of Stephenson LJ at p 301 are worthy of note:

> 'It is also reasonable to believe that the main, although not the only, purpose of section 4 [now s 5 of the 1973 Act] was to protect respondent wives, especially those who had reached middle age, from losing the security, especially the financial security, of being married, and the chance of the benefits which a continuation of the married state would bring them, especially by way of widow's pension rights, on their husbands predeceasing them at not too remote a date. I am not saying that no young, able-bodied wife can hope to succeed in resisting a section 2(1)(e) petition by relying on section 4, or that the loss of the chance of obtaining a state pension, or an army pension, without any adequately compensating provision by the husband, can never be a grave financial hardship to a wife resulting from the dissolution of the marriage which would in all the circumstances be wrong. But it must usually be harder for her . . . to make out the statutory defence . . .'

Although, therefore, the court does not rule out the possibility of this defence succeeding in relation to a younger wife, it will be more difficult for her to succeed than for an older wife.

(c) Quantum of loss

The fact that the benefits which would be lost as a result of the divorce are small will not prevent a wife from succeeding in the use of this defence. This was the case in *Dorrell v Dorrell* [1972] 3 All ER 343, where the loss of widow's pension of £2 per week, to a woman whose total income was £8.25 per week, was considered to be 'as important to her as £100,000 may be to a millionaire, indeed, more important', and as such was considered to be grave financial hardship.

(d) Availability of State benefits

There are two cases in which the availability of State benefits to the wife has been considered.

The first of these was *Dorrell*. The wife opposed the dissolution of the marriage on the ground of grave financial hardship. The husband contended that the wife would be in receipt of supplementary benefit and that, consequently, the loss of her pension rights was a loss to the Department of Health and Social Security and would not result in grave financial hardship to the wife. The court found that the wife would suffer grave financial hardship but that her position must be looked at without taking into account what she received by way of supplementary benefits, and the fact that the wife's pension would go to repay the monies paid to her by the Department was not a reason for excusing the husband from carrying out his obligations to maintain his wife.

Sir George Baker P referred in his judgment to his understanding of the law:

> '. . . which has been applied in these courts for many years in relation to magistrates' orders. The fact that social security is available for a wife is not a reason for a man refusing to carry out, or being excused from carrying out, his obligation to maintain his wife.'

It is, in fact, difficult to see how the husband in *Dorrell* could be accused of seeking to avoid maintaining his wife when the widow's pension which the wife would lose as a result of the divorce would only have been payable in the event of his death.

The court now may well have reached a different decision on the facts of *Dorrell* in the light of the decision of the Court of Appeal in *Delaney v Delaney* [1990] 2 FLR 457, where the court took into account the existence of State benefits available to the wife when deciding what maintenance a husband must pay.

In *Reiterbund v Reiterbund* [1975] 1 All ER 280, the husband contended that a wife would not suffer grave financial hardship, since supplementary benefit to which she would be entitled would not be less than the widow's pension lost on divorce. The wife appealed, contending that in determining whether or not she would suffer grave financial hardship the court was not entitled to take into account her right to social security benefits. The case of *Dorrell* was referred to and Megaw LJ commented, at p 286:

> 'if and insofar as anything which was said in that case ought to be construed to mean that, on the facts such as exist in the present case, the fact and the amount of supplementary benefit must be ignored in assessing financial hardship under section 5, I would respectfully disagree.'

Given that the wife's pension loss would be more than compensated for by the receipt of supplementary benefits, the court could not find that the wife would suffer grave financial hardship and her appeal was dismissed. When reaching his decision in *Reiterbund*, Megaw LJ commented that the facts in *Dorrell* were different from the facts with which he was concerned. The main difference between the two cases is that the benefit that the wife stood to lose in *Reiterbund*, as a result of the divorce, was a widow's benefit, payable from a public fund, and in the absence of that payment she would receive an income from another public fund. In *Dorrell*, the source of the payments the wife would lose was a pension fund into which the husband had made contributions. It is not clear from the judgment in *Reiterbund* whether it was this particular distinction which persuaded the court to take into account the availability of State benefits to the wife.

(e) Conduct

(I) GOOD CONDUCT

The fact that a husband has behaved as generously towards a wife as his circumstances will permit will not prevent a wife from succeeding in her opposition of a dissolution of the marriage on the basis that it would cause her grave financial hardship, if, despite doing his best, the husband is unable to mitigate by a capital payment or by some other means the loss to his wife of a widow's benefit (*Johnson v Johnson* (1982) Fam Law 116).

(II) POOR CONDUCT

The conduct of the parties to the marriage is one of the circumstances which the court must consider when hearing a defence under s 5, and poor conduct on behalf of the wife may prevent her succeeding in her opposition to the granting of a decree, even if the marriage is of reasonable length.

In *Brickell v Brickell* [1973] 3 All ER 508, the parties were married in 1945, when the wife was 30, and separated in 1961. Although the wife subsequently returned to the family home, the parties lived separate and apart. A decree nisi was pronounced on the husband's petition, based on five years' separation and, in granting the decree, the judge gave leave to the wife to apply to the court to rescind the decree nisi should information become available that a widow of the husband would be entitled to receive a pension. It subsequently transpired that, if the wife remained married to the husband and he predeceased her, she would be entitled to a pension of £232 per year. Having found that the wife had suffered grave financial hardship by the loss of the pension, the judge held that, nevertheless, in all the circumstances and, in particular, having regard to the history of the marriage, it would not be wrong to dissolve it. The wife appealed, contending that, having come to the conclusion that she would suffer grave financial hardship, the judge had erred in holding that it would not be wrong to dissolve the marriage and that in coming to his decision he should not have taken into account the fact that the wife had deserted the husband.

On appeal, the court, allowing the decree nisi to stand, held that, in considering the conduct of the parties for the purpose of determining whether it would be wrong to dissolve the marriage, it was bound to have regard to misconduct, ie a matrimonial offence (such as desertion) in the old sense on the part of one of the parties, although the word conduct was not confined to misconduct of that kind.

4.6.2 Section 10 of the Matrimonial Causes Act 1973

4.6.2.1 The statutory provision

There is further limited protection available to a wife under s 10(2) of the 1973 Act, which applies where the petition is based on either the fact of five years' separation or two years' separation with consent and the respondent applies to the court for consideration of his or her financial position after the divorce. Under s 10(3), the court must consider all the circumstances, including age, health, conduct, earning capacity, financial resources and financial obligations of each of the parties, and the financial position of the respondent, as, having regard to the divorce, it is likely to be after the death of the petitioner should the petitioner die first. Subject to s 10(4), the court must not make the decree absolute unless it is satisfied that:

(a) the petitioner should not be required to make any financial provision for the respondent; or
(b) the provision that has been made is reasonable and fair or the best that can be made in the circumstances.

Section 10(4) enables the court to make the decree absolute if it thinks fit, notwithstanding s 10(3), if it appears that there are circumstances making it desirable that the decree should be made absolute without delay and the court has obtained a satisfactory undertaking from the petitioner that he will make such financial provision for the respondent as the court may approve.

The protection offered by s 10 of the 1973 Act is more limited than the protection afforded under s 5. Section 10 is not an absolute bar to divorce. The court is only obliged to satisfy itself that the financial provision is reasonable and fair or the best that can be made in the circumstances, and that may mean that the wife is not fully compensated for lost benefits. Nevertheless, a wife who is able to invoke the protection of s 10 would be in a better position than if she were only able to make applications for the usual financial provision and property adjustment under ss 23 and 24.

So said Ormrod LJ in *Hardy v Hardy* (1981) FLR 321 at p 327:

> 'That leads me to say something about s 10 of the 1973 Act, because it looks as though s 10 is falling into disuse. Section 10(3), which I have already read, is intended to provide a protection to a wife particularly (also to husbands in certain circumstances) who is divorced either on 2 years' separation or on 5 years' separation, and it was put in by Parliament to prevent just this kind of situation arising, namely a divorce against her will at a time highly convenient to the husband financially, and potentially highly prejudicial to her in the future.'

scheme, enquiries should be made about the parties' respective employment histories, the nature of any employment that they may obtain in the future and any period of employment overseas. For example, a husband who is presently unemployed, self-employed or in employment which is not pensionable, may previously have been a member of an occupational pension scheme into which substantial payments have been made on his behalf. Those benefits may have been preserved in the scheme until the date of the husband's retirement, or may have been transferred to a personal pension scheme. Similarly, a woman who is undergoing training to become a teacher may not at that time be accruing pension benefits, but on acquiring a permanent teaching post, she will become a member of the Teachers' Superannuation Scheme and acquire the substantial benefits which attach to such membership. Even where the husband is unemployed and has not previously been a member of an occupational pension scheme, the State scheme should not be overlooked.

It is important to look beyond information obtained specifically for the purpose of considering pension rights for clues about whether full disclosure of all pension entitlement has been given. It may be necessary to make further enquiries. For example, where the husband is a director with a 20 per cent or greater interest in his company, enquiries should be made as to whether a small self-administered scheme is in existence (see **2.4**).

If it is the wife's second marriage, it may be relevant to ascertain what, if any, pension benefits she acquired by virtue of her first marriage and then lost as a result of her second marriage. For example, widow's benefits acquired upon the death of a spouse may be extinguished on remarriage, even if the later marriage is subsequently dissolved or annulled where the marriage was voidable rather than void (*Ward v Secretary of State for Social Services* [1990] 1 FLR 119). Automatic extinction is now less common than was previously the case, but is still possible.

It may also be appropriate to enquire as to the parties' medical condition; this may be of importance when looking at what form of insurance may be necessary in the future and the likely cost of obtaining such cover. For example, a man who has a history of heart disease will find it almost impossible to obtain further life cover, other than at prohibitive rates. This will therefore increase the importance and value of any life insurance which is already secured against his life.

5.1.3 Nature of pension schemes

The nature of the pension scheme or schemes of which the parties are, or have been, members will affect the type of information to be sought regarding those schemes and the source of that information. For example, if the only pension benefits are those under the State pension scheme, it will probably not be necessary to seek much further information. In contrast, if the husband is a member of a small self-administered scheme, the individual nature of such a scheme may necessitate a detailed enquiry, not only as to the likely benefits available under the scheme, but also as to the assets in which monies have been invested.

5.1.4 Strategy for discovery

Once the status of the parties and the types of schemes involved have been established, deciding what information to obtain concerning those schemes and the best source of that information should become a less daunting prospect. Developing a strategy should help to avoid the incurrence of unnecessary costs whilst also ensuring that all necessary information is obtained. Consideration should first be given to the type of information that is available under the type of scheme in question and then to the most expeditious and cost-effective means of obtaining that information.

Although the usual course of action is to make a request of the other party pursuant to the Family Proceedings Rules 1991, r 2.63, it may also be possible to obtain the relevant information directly from the trustees or managers of the pension scheme. Some information must be disclosed to the spouse of the pension-scheme member upon request; other information can be made available only with the member's consent. Bypassing the procedure under r 2.63 in this way may save substantial costs and time; it may also help to ensure that the information provided is correct and that no information is withheld. If the r 2.63 procedure is adopted, and the requested party fails to produce the information on the grounds that he is unable to obtain it, establishing the amount of information to which a scheme member is entitled will assist the practitioner in considering whether all necessary steps have been taken to obtain the information sought (see *G v G (Financial Provision: Discovery)* [1992] 1 FLR 40).

The type of information available, who is entitled to that information, and to whom a request should be made for such information, will depend on the scheme under consideration.

5.1.5 The State pension scheme

The limited benefits available under the State pension scheme and its inflexible nature means that there is relatively little information that needs to be obtained in order to ascertain the benefits which may be lost and for which compensation may be required.

5.1.5.1 What information to seek

The most important information to obtain is the amount and period of National Insurance contributions made by both parties during their working lives (see **1.2.1**). If the wife does not satisfy the conditions for a flat-rate pension, it will be important to ascertain whether she will be entitled to such a pension by virtue of her husband's contributions. Other information, such as whether either party has elected to defer receipt of the pension and whether either party has contracted out of SERPS (see **1.2.1**), may also be relevant.

5.1.5.2 Where to obtain the information

All of the relevant information will be contained in a pensions forecast that the DSS will issue upon request to a woman aged under 59 years 8 months or a man aged under 64 years 8 months. In order to obtain a forecast of a party's entitlement to a flat-rate pension and any additional SERPS benefit, Form BR19 (see Appendix, precedent 12), which can be obtained from any DSS office, should be completed and returned to the address stated on the form. Until such time as a decree nisi is made absolute, a wife has no right to obtain details of her husband's entitlement under the State pension scheme from the DSS. If, however, the husband gives his consent, it may be possible to obtain that information direct from the DSS. The wife would, of course, be entitled to obtain a forecast of her entitlement based upon her own contributions. Once the decree nisi has been made absolute, the DSS will issue a pensions forecast direct to the former wife; this will include details of her former husband's substituted contributions.

5.1.6 Occupational pension schemes

5.1.6.1 What information to seek

The most important information to seek will usually be a statement of the amount of benefit payable to a member of a scheme upon his retirement, whether by way of lump sum or pension, and what widow's and dependants' benefits are payable in the event of the member's death either prior to, or after retirement. Such information is fundamental when considering what benefits will be lost as a result of the divorce. However, it should not be sought in isolation. Information concerning the scheme itself may give a greater insight into the benefits that have been or may be lost, and the most appropriate way of securing compensation for that loss. Although the cost of obtaining such information should always be borne in mind and balanced against the likely benefits that it may produce, the following information may be sought:

(a) a copy of the trust deeds and rules;
(b) explanatory guides for members or other documents that are available;
(c) an estimate of the transfer value of the member's benefits;
(d) the trustees' annual report and accounts;
(e) an actuarial valuation report.

Explanatory guides, which are usually produced for the benefit of members and their dependants, are likely to be the most useful source of information for the family law practitioner. It is important to establish that the explanatory booklet and the benefits it describes are up to date. The definition of a spouse for the purposes of the scheme should be established (ie whether it includes a spouse living apart from her husband) and it is also important to establish whether there is an option available to the husband to make nominations in respect of benefits arising under the scheme upon his death.

It may be appropriate to make a specific enquiry of the trustees to ascertain whether they tend to favour a present wife in place of a former wife when exercising their discretion. There is, however, no need for the trustees to disclose their deliberations about their exercise of discretion; but if reasons are disclosed then they may be challenged (*Re Londonderry's Settlement, Peat v Walsh* [1965] Ch 918).

5.1.6.2 The Disclosure of Information Regulations

The right of a member of a pension scheme to obtain information concerning that scheme has been extended by the Occupational Pension Schemes (Disclosure of Information) Regulations 1986 (SI 1986/1046, as amended by SI 1986/1717). The Regulations specify the information which trustees or managers of a scheme are obliged to provide, to whom and when that information must be provided, and whether that information should be made available only on request or whether it should be automatically provided. A good working knowledge of the information available under the Regulations, and who is entitled to that information, should prove invaluable, whether that information is to be sought direct or through the other party under r 2.63.

Regulation 4: constitution of the scheme

Copies of all trust deeds, rules and deeds of amendment, including the names of participating employers, should be provided upon request to:

(a) members and prospective members (ie people entitled to join in the future);
(b) spouses of members and prospective members; and
(c) beneficiaries of members under the scheme.

If copy documents are requested, a reasonable fee may be charged, but inspection of documents must be allowed free of charge at all reasonable hours. The request for such information must be made in writing; it must be complied with unless it is made within one year of an earlier such request by the same member.

Regulation 5: scheme details

The type of information that has to be provided under reg 5 includes:

(a) the benefits payable and how they are calculated;
(b) which benefits are discretionary;
(c) any conditions to which payment of benefit is subject;
(d) the method used to calculate members' and employers' contributions;
(e) whether there is power to increase pensions in payment and, if so, who can exercise that power and whether it is discretionary.

The information specified in reg 5 must be provided automatically to members joining the scheme after 31 October 1987 within 13 weeks of their joining the scheme, and must be provided to spouses of members and prospective members and other beneficiaries under the scheme upon written request. Such a request cannot be made more than once every three years.

Regulation 6: information for individuals

The information available under reg 6 includes benefit statements, statements about death benefits and options, and early leaver statements.

A benefit statement should include the amount of benefit payable and, where a payment is made periodically, the conditions on which payment will be continued and any provisions under which the amount payable may be altered. It must also specify the amount of the member's own benefits and of his or her survivor's benefits payable from normal pension age or later death, whether that amount is calculated as if his or her service ended on the date of the statement or as if his or her service were to continue to normal pension age without regard to future salary increases; or specify the method by which those amounts may be calculated and give sufficient information about past salary contributions and years of service to enable the calculation to be made. A benefit statement must be given to members and beneficiaries automatically when a benefit becomes payable or as soon as possible afterwards but prior to a benefit becoming payable. A member may request a benefit statement no more than once a year. Members of a money purchase scheme must be provided with a benefit statement automatically once a year and are not entitled to request one during the intervening period.

Statements about death benefits and options must be given automatically, when a member or beneficiary dies, to anyone over 18 who has rights under the scheme. The information must be given to a personal representative or someone authorised to act on behalf of the person entitled to the rights as soon as practicable after receipt of a request from them. Such a request cannot be made more than once every three years.

Early leaver statements, which provide information concerning the rights and options available to a person leaving a scheme before retirement age, must be given upon receipt of a request from a member and, automatically, at the end of the member's service. A request for such information cannot be made more than once a year.

Other information which can be obtained by virtue of the Regulations includes trustees' annual reports and actuarial annual reports. It is, however, unlikely that such information will be of general assistance except in exceptional cases.

5.1.6.3 Pension tracing service

The Register of Occupational and Personal Pension schemes was established by the Social Security Act 1990. The purpose of the register is to assist individuals to trace their preserved pension benefits from the pension schemes of former employers. The register will only enable a potential beneficiary to trace, for example, the identity of those administering the pension scheme of a known former employee. A search cannot be made by a wife by reference to her husband's name to indicate the schemes of which he is a member.

Anyone who is, may be, or may become entitled to benefit under a former pension scheme, or any person acting on the beneficiary's behalf, may make a 'tracing request' (on Form PR4: see Appendix, precedent 14) by applying to the Registrar of Pension Schemes, Occupational Pensions Board, PO Box 1NN, Newcastle-Upon-Tyne NE99 1NN, tel: 091-22-56393/4). A separate request must be made in relation to each scheme.

Initially, the information available on the register will relate to schemes established before 1 May 1991. Trustees of all registrable schemes must provide information to the registrar and pay a levy in respect of all current schemes to fund the establishment and the upkeep of the register.

Information on the register will comprise the name (and former name(s)) of the scheme, its address, its status (ie current, paid-up or closed), the year it was established, the names of the trustees and the scheme administrator, details of the principal employer and employers associated with the scheme, and the name, address and telephone number of a contact.

The tracing service covers all occupational and personal pension schemes, whether current or paid-up and public service pension schemes.

5.1.7 Small self-administered schemes

5.1.7.1 Where to obtain the information

Although the Regulations do not apply to small self-administered schemes (see **2.4**), where a pension scheme is approved by the Pensions Scheme Office (PSO), written particulars of all essential features of the scheme which concern him must be provided in writing to every employee who is, or has a right to be, a member of the scheme (FA 1970, s 19(2)(b)). Therefore, the statutory information concerning small self-administered schemes which has to be made available is limited both in terms of the type of information to be disclosed and the people who are entitled to request such information. It may, therefore, be necessary to look to the equitable rights to information which are available.

As small self-administered schemes must be established through a trust deed and rules, it may be possible to use the law of trusts to obtain information concerning the scheme. There is a substantial body of law, for example *Chaine-Nickson v Bank of Ireland* [1976] IR 393, relating to trustees' obligations to give information to or make information available to members where the word 'member' is used instead of the technical legal term of 'beneficiary'. In the absence of special circumstances, a trust member is entitled to production and inspection of all trust documents in the possession of the trustees, which includes title deeds and other documents relating to the title to the trust property and the nature and content of the member's own beneficial interest. If the trustee is unable to supply information direct to a member, he must indicate where the member can obtain it. Other persons, such as wives and dependants, may be included in the right to information even though they are not strictly members. A detailed study of the relevant trust law is, however, outside the scope of this book.

As the directors of a company are the sole or principal members of a small self-administered scheme, and also normally act as the scheme's trustees, any such director should be able to supply such information as is required concerning the scheme.

5.1.7.2 What information to seek

The trust deed may contain details of the level of contributions to be made both by the company and the individual director. A copy of the trust deed should therefore be obtained. If the trust deed does not contain any such information, a copy of any separate agreement between the individual director and the company should be sought.

It will usually be of assistance to seek the identity of the assets in which the scheme has invested, as such information will give an indication as to the value of the assets and the amount of future provision they may be expected to produce for the scheme and members. For example, the assets may take the form of office premises, where the beneficiary of the scheme is a company director in a closed company.

Finally, the actuarial reports on investment which have to be submitted by the trustees to the PSO every three years may provide a valuable source of information about the scheme.

Other means of obtaining information concerning the pension scheme may be through the Employment Protection (Consolidation) Act 1978, s 1(3)(d)(ii) and the Social Security Pensions Act 1975, ss 56A and 56E, which entitle a member of a pension scheme to obtain information about that scheme from his employer.

5.1.8 Retirement Annuity Contracts and Personal Pension Schemes

The differences between retirement annuity contracts and personal pension schemes have been considered in Chapter 2 at **2.5.1**. The many similarities, however, are highlighted when consideration is given to what information should be obtained in relation to both types of policies.

5.1.8.1 What information to seek

Retirement annuity contracts and personal pension schemes are both taken out as a contract between an individual and a provider of pensions – usually an insurance company.

Once the identity of the provider is known, the information to seek concerning the policy falls into the following general categories:

- the contributions that have been made to the policy;
- the amount of benefits that are likely to become payable under the policy;
- to whom the benefits will be payable;
- when they will become payable.

Each can be taken in turn.

Contributions

When seeking the information concerning the contributions which have been made into the policy, it should be borne in mind that both regular instalments and one-off payments can be made into both retirement annuity contracts and personal pension schemes, although contributions from employers are only allowed under personal pension schemes. It should not, therefore, be assumed that regular payments made by a member are the only contributions that have been made to a policy. The fact that personal pension schemes can accept funds from other approved schemes should also be borne in mind. Heavy, single contributions at or around the time of separation may prompt other considerations in ancillary relief applications, such as an application under s 37 of MCA 1973 for the payment to be set aside on the basis that it is a reviewable disposition. In order for such an application to succeed, the court must be satisfied that the payment was made to a third party with the intention of defeating the application of a party bringing ancillary relief proceedings, or impeding the enforcement of any order which may be, or has been made, in those proceedings. If the disposition is made within three years before the date of the application, it is presumed, unless the contrary is shown, that it was made with the intention of defeating the other party's claim to financial relief. However, if the third party to whom the disposition was made took it in good faith, without any notice to defeat the claim for financial relief, the court has no power to set aside the disposition.

Benefits payable

As both retirement annuity contracts and personal pension schemes are money purchase schemes (see Glossary), benefits are based upon the investment performance of the fund and not upon final salary. Obtaining an accurate forecast of the level of benefits payable under the scheme may therefore prove more difficult, the value not being immediately ascertainable. The provider of the pension will, however, be able to provide an indication of the possible benefits that might be paid under the policy under rules laid down by LAUTRO (see Glossary). Those rules lay down two bases on which future benefits may be illustrated, the higher illustration representing the rate of return of 13 per cent per annum in the period up to retirement and 10 per cent thereafter, and the lower illustration representing the rate of return of 8.5 per cent per annum in the period up to retirement and 8 per cent per annum thereafter. These two amounts do not represent the upper and lower limits of the possible amount of the benefit. The type of benefits available both on death in service and death during retirement should also be ascertained. See Chapter 2.

To whom?
In addition to the policyholder, his dependants may be entitled to benefits under the scheme. Although benefits cannot be assigned during the policyholder's lifetime, they can be put in trust for dependants on death. The policyholder can usually direct that the entire fund should be paid to a single beneficiary immediately on his death, or that the fund should be paid to a trustee who will have a discretion to appoint the fund to any one or more of a class of potential beneficiaries. There are no restrictions on the class of potential beneficiaries so that policies can be written in trust to former spouses or adult children.

When they become payable?
The main difference between a retirement annuity contract and a personal pension scheme is the age at which benefits may be taken (see Chapter 2 at **2.5.1**). Enquiries should therefore be made in order to ascertain whether a policyholder has chosen a retirement date and whether he has elected to take a tax-free lump sum from the fund which has accumulated up to that date. The projected value of any such lump sum that is available should be obtained.

5.1.8.2 How to obtain the required information

Information concerning the type of benefits available under a particular policy, and when such benefits can be withdrawn, is usually clearly ascertainable from the policyholder's policy document. This should have been supplied to the policyholder when the contract was taken out and therefore should be readily obtainable under the Family Proceedings Rules 1991, r 2.63 procedure. If the original policy document is not in the policyholder's possession, he may have a copy available. If, however, the policy document has been lost, it should be possible to obtain a duplicate from the provider of the pension, although the procedure can be complicated and will usually involve the policyholder in having to give an indemnity in order to be able to make a claim under the policy.

Forecasts of the value of the benefits payable under the policy, details of any nominations or declarations of trust which have been made and the amount of the contributions made into the policy, should be available upon request by the policyholder. Such information is not available as of right to anyone other than the policyholder, although the policy provider may be prepared to disclose such information to a third party upon the authority of the policyholder.

5.1.9 Unapproved schemes and arrangements

Unapproved schemes are uncommon and may prove to be the most difficult to identify and obtain sufficient information about. If it is suspected that an unapproved scheme exists, a copy of the employee's contract of employment may confirm its existence. Otherwise, a direct question concerning the existence of any such scheme should be asked. The benefits payable under such a scheme should be ascertained.

5.2 VALUATION

The process of discovery, as discussed above, should reveal what pension benefits are available to both parties and what benefits would be lost by either party as a result of divorce. Although the value of the benefits lost will usually be apparent following discovery, the cost of replacing those lost benefits may be considerably more difficult to ascertain.

The first distinction to make is between the benefits to which a widow would have been entitled in her own right and her loss of opportunity in sharing in her husband's own benefits. The cost of replacing the death-in-service element of a pension should be relatively easy to ascertain, for example by means of obtaining a quotation for a term-life policy to cover the future needs of the wife (see **3.3.4**). Actuarial techniques can be applied to estimate the cost of replacing widows' benefits under a pension scheme. The most difficult exercise is valuing the loss of opportunity of sharing a husband's own benefits.

If there is to be a continuing maintenance obligation, the amount of pension to which the husband will be entitled upon retirement will be taken into account when the appropriate level of maintenance payable is considered at the time of retirement. If, however, there is to be a 'clean break', some effort may need to be made to put a value upon the loss of enjoying such benefits. When acting for the husband, however, it is important to ensure that the loss of enjoyment of these benefits is not, in effect, double counted. This may occur if the level of lump sum payable is calculated by reference to the death of the payee and an additional sum included by way of compensation for loss of enjoyment of retirement benefits. Any tax-free lump sum available to the husband upon retirement should also be taken into consideration, although the consequent reduction in the level of pension payments should not be overlooked.

The second distinction to make is between the value of benefits lost as at the date of divorce and the value of benefits available upon retirement. It is often the case that the wife's greatest need for capital arises at the time of divorce, usually to rehouse herself. This distinction is relevant not only in terms of the source from which valuation advice should be obtained, based upon differing points of valuation, but also on the issue of whether the wife will benefit from post-divorce pension contributions and increases in pensionable pay. Current case-law offers no guidence as to whether only pension rights which have accrued up to the date of divorce are relevant. The court therefore retains a discretion as with any other type of asset. The court's discretion may be influenced in one direction by the divorce taking place after a lengthy period of separation or in the other by the existence of young children in the care of the wife.

Problems may arise, however, if the husband is only able to make capital available upon his retirement. If the appropriate point of valuation is considered to be the date of the divorce, an actuary may be instructed to value the lost benefits. (See Appendix, precedent 13 for a letter of instruction.). However, a consulting actuary who is willing to assist may prove difficult to find, particularly one who is prepared to undertake the work at a level of remuneration that can be justified in the context of the costs of the case. Suitable actuaries may be found in the major firms of insurance brokers. The results produced by two different actuaries instructed in the same case may be completely different. This will generally be due to the different assumptions being adopted by them. It would therefore be advisable, where possible, for any two actuaries instructed by opposing parties in a case to agree the assumptions to be adopted.

If the lost benefits to be valued are those which would be available upon retirement, a pensions consultant may be the appropriate person to instruct. Again, the cost of obtaining such advice should be ascertained beforehand and balanced against the likely benefits arising from the availability of such information within the context of the case. Alternatively, if the pension is a money purchase scheme, the projections produced by the insurance company may be capable of agreement between the parties.

If the information obtained, either from an actuary or pensions consultant, needs to be presented to the court on a contested ancillary relief hearing, it will constitute expert evidence. The provisions of CCR Ord 20, rr 27 and 28 govern procedure on the admissibility of expert evidence. It should therefore be borne in mind that, in the absence of agreement, leave will be required to adduce expert evidence. Booth J's comments in *Evans v Evans* [1990] 1 FLR 319, that all professional witnesses should be careful to avoid a partisan approach and maintain proper professional standards, should also be borne in mind.

CHAPTER 6

LEGAL FRAMEWORK: SOLUTIONS

6.1 INTRODUCTION

Having secured sufficient information about the pension schemes involved and obtained appropriate expert advice, the practitioner will be faced with a daunting amount of material from which he must extract the right solution. It may be very tempting to give up at this stage and to treat loss of pension rights as nothing more than a make-weight, but a strategy should be developed to make the best use of the assembled information.

6.1.1 Four questions

The strategy suggested is to ask four questions from which a series of possible solutions should emerge.

6.1.1.1 What are the losses involved?

The reader will by now be familiar with the various types of loss of pension rights which a wife may sustain on divorce. In the individual case, it is worth preparing a schedule summarising the losses in relation to each scheme involved, indicating any valuations obtained.

6.1.1.2 What are the needs of the person being compensated?

Consideration should be given to whether the wife needs compensation for loss of pension rights at all. For example, compensation may be inappropriate in the case of a short marriage and/or where 'the time when [the pension] will fall to hand is so remote that it has little relevance except as a piece of background' (*Hedges v Hedges* [1991] 1 FLR 196, per Mustill LJ at p 198). It is interesting to note that in *Hedges*, where the parties had been married for four-and-a-half years prior to separation, the husband was 41 and the wife 37. It is submitted that, in view of the parties' ages, the court may well have reached a different view had the marriage been longer.

It is worthwhile considering whether the wife already has her own pension scheme or whether she is about to enter pensionable employment.

It will also be important to look at the overall structure of any settlement of a wife's claim for ancillary relief. If a wife is to receive continuing maintenance under a consent order, then compensation for loss of a widow's pension would seem reasonable. If, however, she is to receive capitalised maintenance as a lump sum under the *Duxbury* principle, then there may be an element of double compensation if she is also given capitalised compensation for loss of pension rights.

Regard must be paid to timing: it is important to consider when the compensation will be needed. Is a lump sum required now or continuing provision in the longer term? A wife may have a specific need for immediate capital, for example, for rehousing or to make an additional voluntary contribution to her own pension fund or she may elect to purchase a deferred annuity. On the other hand, the wife's concern may centre upon continuing income provision, which may dictate an insurance-based solution.

6.1.1.3 How can the loss and the needs be matched?

The answer to this question will lead to the choice of an appropriate solution. However, one must not lose sight of the fact that one is concerned not only with the needs of the person being compensated but also the ability of the husband to provide that compensation. In many situations, it will be recognised at a relatively early stage that the whole process is something of an academic exercise.

The practitioner must be wary of being overprecise in what is, after all, a discretionary jurisdiction. Valuations are simply a means to an end and the search for the right solution should always be viewed in the broader context of MCA 1973, s 25.

6.1.1.4 Is the solution to be implemented by settlement or court order?

Before the appropriate solution can be identified, an overriding consideration will be the framework within which the problem is to be tackled.

In a contested hearing resulting in a court order, the solutions are limited to the powers of the court under MCA 1973, ss 23 and 24. The court has no power to order a party to take out a life assurance policy (*Milne v Milne* (1981) FLR 286) or to make a payment to a third party, eg into the wife's existing pension scheme (*Burton v Burton and Another* [1986] 2 FLR 419). A lump sum order may, of course, be of use, and an order for secured provision will at least ensure that periodical payments extend beyond the death of the payer up to the death or remarriage of the payee, but both these solutions depend upon the availability of capital. The court may order that the level of periodical payments for the wife may be suitably adjusted so as to enable her to make pension provision for herself. It may well be, however, that the wife is left with no alternative but to rely upon her rights under the Inheritance (Provision for Family and Dependants) Act 1975. Caution should be exercised in including an order under s 15 of the 1975 Act in a consent order when the pension problem remains unresolved.

If the solution is to be implemented by an agreement which is to be incorporated into a consent order, this will provide a totally flexible range of solutions. It will be important to ensure that matters which fall outside the jurisdiction of the court are suitably incorporated into the consent order by way of undertakings or agreements (see *Livesey (Formerly Jenkins) v*

Jenkins [1985] FLR 813). Thus, it will be possible to formulate an insurance-based solution or one involving contracts to leave property by will.

6.1.2 Categories of solutions

Having addressed the four questions referred to above, four broad categories of solutions emerge:

(a) loss avoidance – staying married;
(b) immediate compensation for loss of pension benefits;
(c) deferred compensation for loss of pension benefits;
(d) compensation for loss of death benefits.

Each of these solutions can be addressed in turn.

6.2 LOSS AVOIDANCE – STAYING MARRIED

Avoiding divorce altogether is rarely a complete and satisfactory solution. This solution might be suitable for parties approaching retirement age where neither party wishes to remarry. For a couple set on divorce, it should be regarded as a last resort. It is, however, essential to consider it at an early stage when taking instructions. If a practitioner is acting for a wife in a case with a substantial pension element, proceedings for divorce should not be issued until it has been considered as an alternative.

Divorce avoidance is not a panacea. All it does is preserve the status of the wife as a widow in the event of her husband's death, so that she remains entitled to his death-in-service benefits and the widow's pension. If the husband remains alive, the wife has no automatic access to the husband's retirement benefits during his lifetime. Therefore, when considering this solution, the practitioner must look at priorities. If both the wife and the husband really want a divorce, is the preservation of widow's benefits really a good enough reason for not having a divorce? To not issue proceedings may not be a complete solution – a wife may find herself presented with an unreasonable behaviour or adultery petition which she cannot later resist. Further, the other assets may not be distributed as efficiently without divorce proceedings.

However, if staying married is felt to be a suitable option, what is the best structure to use?

6.2.1 Deed of separation

A deed of separation has the advantage of enabling the parties to agree a settlement dealing with all the assets as if there were divorce proceedings, but it does, of course, require consensus.

If there is no divorce and the assets are divided by way of a deed of separation, no specific provision for the preservation of widow's rights is needed in the deed. However, there are a few points to consider.

(a) Some pension schemes include a clause providing that widow's benefits are paid only if the couple are 'married and living together' at the time of the husband's death. It is therefore essential to look at the rules of the scheme to check that the widow will not lose her pension on this ground. Some schemes give the trustees a wide discretion about whether a widow's pension should be paid; others give the husband a right to choose whether a widow's pension is payable.

(b) Even if the wife has access to a widow's pension on the husband's death, she may not automatically be entitled to his death-in-service benefits. The pension scheme may provide that the husband has to make a nomination to the trustees of the pension scheme about what should happen to death-in-service benefits. Without a nomination, death-in-service benefits may fall into his estate and be distributed in accordance with his will.

(c) The husband may need to agree, as part of the settlement, to pay future contributions to the scheme to ensure that the widow's pension is preserved or enhanced so that she will have sufficient to live on in the event of his death. The practitioner should, therefore, ensure that the scheme is sufficiently funded.

(d) The husband may be able to allocate benefits on his retirement which will have the effect of reducing the widow's pension. For example, he may elect on retirement to take a larger lump sum and a larger pension for himself during his retirement.

Clauses in the deed of separation may therefore be required to deal with these difficulties, but the husband's co-operation is, of course, essential.

Finally, the client should be advised that a deed of separation is no bar to later divorce proceedings. Even if the structure of the financial settlement made on separation is upheld within divorce proceedings, that does not stop the wife losing her widow's benefit once the decree absolute is made.

6.2.2. Judicial separation

Judicial separation is not a bar to a later divorce, but it has the obvious advantage that a solution can be imposed by the court and the wife still remains the widow for the purposes of a pension scheme.

The points to watch for in relation to deeds of separation (see **6.2.1**) also apply to judicial separation. The solution may still be dependent upon the husband co-operating and being willing to give undertakings. Pressure can of course be put upon the husband to give appropriate undertakings or else suffer the consequences of a harsher order.

Remember that no final financial order can be made on judicial separation – the clean break does not apply; MCA 1973, s 25A applies only in relation to divorce and nullity.

6.2.3 Other court proceedings

There are other court proceedings which may be of use where a divorce is not wanted and judicial separation is not appropriate. The practitioner might consider the use of the following legislation:

(a) Law of Property Act 1925, s 30 – for sale of property held under trust for sale;
(b) Married Women's Property Act 1882 – for declarations about ownership and orders for sale of land and other property;
(c) MCA 1973, s 27 – right to apply for maintenance and a lump sum during the marriage, based on husband's failure to provide reasonable maintenance.

6.2.4 Postponing the decree absolute

It may be appropriate for there to be divorce proceedings but for the couple to stay technically married in order to preserve pension benefits.

6.2.4.1 Postponing decree absolute until a solution is found

Section 10 of MCA 1973 has been dealt with at length in Chapter 4 at **4.6.2**. Section 10 is only available where the wife is the respondent to a petition based on the fact of a two or five years' separation. It is not an absolute bar to the divorce but merely preserves the marriage (and therefore the widow's pension rights) until the best available solution is found.

It may be possible for a petitioner to postpone the decree absolute by resisting a respondent's application on notice under MCA 1973, s 9(2). A district judge is not bound to make the decree nisi absolute unless he is satisfied as to the matters listed in FPR 1991, r 2.49(2). For example, there may be outstanding ancillary relief proceedings (*Smith v Smith* [1990] 1 FLR 438).

6.2.4.2 Postponement of decree absolute until the husband retires

In some cases it may be possible to agree with the husband that either the whole of the divorce or the decree absolute should be postponed until after the husband's retirement date.

Whether this is worthwhile will depend upon the exact wording of the pension scheme. Some schemes will still pay a widow's pension if the husband and wife divorce after retirement; of these some may specify that the widow's pension is payable only if the husband and wife were married and living together at the date of retirement, others simply require that the husband and wife should be married at the date of retirement. In appropriate cases involving a smaller pension scheme (for example in a small self-administered scheme), it may be possible to persuade the trustees to change the wording of the scheme by resolving to pay a widow's pension in either of the above circumstances.

It must be emphasised again that it is essential to look at the rules of the scheme in question before deciding on a course of action.

6.2.4.3 The absolute bar: Matrimonial Causes Act 1973, section 5

Section 5 of the MCA 1973 has been fully dealt with in Chapter 4 at **4.6.1**. It should be used as a solution only where all else fails and no other solution is suitable. It must be remembered that it is only available to the respondent to a petition based on five years' separation. For the wife's adviser to rely on s 5 alone as a way of preserving a widow's pension is a risky course of action. It is very much a last resort and other more constructive solutions should be explored.

If the wife succeeds in her argument under s 5 and is able to persuade the court that she will suffer 'grave financial hardship' and that therefore a decree absolute should not be granted, it will then become necessary to negotiate a settlement based on a deed of separation or a judicial separation.

6.3 IMMEDIATE COMPENSATION FOR LOSS OF PENSION BENEFITS

During the 1980s, and particularly since the passing of MFPA 1984, the courts have exhorted practitioners to find immediate and final solutions in the form of clean-break settlements. Pension rights are the enemy of the clean-break principle. The enthusiasm for imposing clean breaks in recent years has contributed to the neglect of former wives' entitlement to share in their former husbands' pension schemes. However, for those who can afford a properly worked out, carefully calculated clean break settlement, it remains the ideal solution. It compensates for loss of both retirement benefits and death benefits.

In this section, the ways in which court orders can be used to provide compensation for all types of lost pension rights are considered. The suggested solutions are only a series of ideas – ingenuity is required to find a solution which fits the facts of an individual case.

6.3.1 Property adjustment orders

Property adjustment orders cannot be used to order a husband to transfer his pension scheme entitlement direct to a wife. Pension rights on retirement are non-assignable.

Rights under occupational schemes are personal to the member of the scheme, and an order requiring the husband to transfer benefits or contingent benefits will normally cause automatic revocation of his own rights to that pension. Most trust deeds and rules contain a clause (sometimes known as a 'spendthrift clause') stating that any attempt to charge, assign or pledge a pension will lead to loss of rights. The valuable tax concessions available for pension schemes are allowed so that people can provide themselves with retirement benefits, not so that they can use their pension schemes to settle their debts. The problem of the spendthrift clause was considered in *Edmonds v Edmonds* [1965] 1 All ER 379, where the husband was in receipt of a pension from his employment by a petroleum company and an attachment of earnings order against his pension receipts triggered an automatic revocation. The same considerations apply in the case of both retirement annuity contracts and personal pension schemes – they will invariably contain clauses against non-assignment.

Property adjustment orders can therefore only be used to transfer other assets in compensation for lost pension rights. It is common practice to treat a husband's pension scheme as a make-weight and to use it as an argument for giving a wife a larger share of other assets such as the matrimonial home. Although better than nothing, the method is often used unscientifically without giving proper consideration to what is being given up and for what future needs provision is being made.

6.3.1.1 The matrimonial home

In some circumstances, the family home may be treated as a source of a future pension, as could any asset which can be realised for cash. For example, an outright transfer of the house to the wife on the basis that she could sell it, 'trade down' to a smaller property, and invest the extra capital for her retirement might be possible if proper calculations are carried out to determine what income she might realise by investing the money thereby released. This issue is dealt with below in connection with the use by the wife of capital received from a lump sum order.

6.3.1.2 Endowment insurance policies

Endowment insurance policies are not like pensions; they can be assigned and they can therefore be the subject of a property adjustment order. Like pension benefits, they will be worth more at maturity than they are worth at the time of settlement and they may be suitable property to use as compensation for lost pension benefits.

It may also be worthwhile to consider the possibility of funding a new endowment insurance policy rather than transferring an existing one. The husband would undertake, as part of the overall settlement, to pay the premiums on an endowment policy to yield a lump sum at a date in the future – perhaps on his or his wife's retirement from employment.

A few practical points deserve mention.

(a) Many people have endowment policies only as additional security for a mortgage. Assignment of such a policy will not be possible unless alternative security arrangements are made.
(b) For a policy not used as security for a loan, the consent of the insurance company is not required for transfer of the policy. A standard form of assignment of the policy is included in the Appen-

dix, precedent 11, but remember that many insurance companies insist on using their own forms.

(c) An assignment of an insurance policy from the husband to the wife does not create a liability to capital gains tax, but it should be noted that the wife who was not the original policyholder may find herself liable to capital gains tax on the profit element when she benefits under the policy on maturity or subsequent disposal (Taxation of Chargeable Gains Act 1992, s 210). If s 210 applies, it is important to ensure that the transfer takes place after decree absolute or after the end of the tax year of separation so that the wife acquires the policy at the base value at the date of transfer (see **3.3.1**).

(d) Provision must be made for payment of continuing premiums whether by the husband or the wife. Difficulties may arise if undertakings to pay premiums are not coterminous with a wife's right to receive maintenance. For example, if a husband undertakes to pay premiums during the term of a policy, he may still be doing so even after the wife has remarried. Undertakings should therefore be carefully drafted to ensure that they precisely follow the wishes of the parties.

(e) Surrendering a life insurance policy should be seen as a last resort. The loss of benefits on surrender means that the premiums have given a poor return as an investment. Before surrendering, one should consider other options. First, it may be possible to sell the life insurance policy, particularly older ones. This can be done through a number of agencies (e.g. Beale Dobie & Co, tel 0621 851133; Foster & Cranfield, tel 071-608 1941). Policies may be auctioned, although by no means all policies have a market value which is higher than the surrender value. Alternatively, a policy may be disposed of through a market-maker, such as Policy Register Ltd, tel 061-763-1919. Secondly, it may be possible to obtain from the life insurance company a loan based on the surrender value. Some companies may even be prepared to roll up the interest during the term of the loan, which would usually be the same as the policy. Whilst one should always beware of rolling-up interest, because of the way the expense accelerates, this may be helpful on marriage breakdown. The interest rate will probably be similar to that offered by building societies and banks, but may be more advantageous.

Where insurance policies are held in trust, the court's powers under MCA 1973, s 24(1)(c) and (d) to vary ante-nuptial or post-nuptial settlements are worth bearing in mind. The courts have given a wide interpretation to the meaning of ante-nuptial and post-nuptial settlements. As has been mentioned in Chapter 3, the trusts under MWPA 1882, s 11 fall within s 24 and can be varied. Particular care should be given during disclosure to finding out what trust arrangements may be in existence. Orders would need to be drafted accordingly if the benefit of a life insurance policy is to be redirected from one spouse to the other.

6.3.1.3 Business premises

Cases involving, for example, family companies or farms, may allow possibilities for providing capital which can then be used to supply an income. Whilst courts are reluctant to order a sale of business premises, since these provide income for the family, an alternative solution may be to transfer such property to the wife, who could then lease those premises back to the husband. This would enable the husband to continue with his business, whilst at the same time, under the terms of a lease, the wife would receive rent, either at an agreed rate or at the market rate. If the lease is granted for a term that would end upon the husband's retirement, the wife would remain in possession of the business premises, then either sell them or let them at a market rent to another tenant. These arrangements will only be possible in limited circumstances, and may be impossible if the husband is in partnership with third parties.

6.3.2 Lump sum orders

An immediate lump sum order for payment of cash at the time of divorce to compensate for benefits which will be denied on retirement or death has many advantages over deferred provision. It provides certainty for both husband and wife, leaving them to make independent, long-term financial planning. It avoids the need to consider what will happen if the husband dies before taking his pension or paying a deferred lump sum. Unfortunately, it is also too expensive for most people who may not have sufficient income and capital to house themselves and pay the bills at the time of the divorce, let alone find an extra sum of capital to invest for the future.

For the majority of people, deferred payments (as dealt with below) are the more obvious solution. But where there is sufficient capital for an immediate clean break, how should the problem be tackled?

The academic exercise of valuing what pension entitlement a wife is giving up is important, but it is far more important to work out how her practical needs are to be met on retirement. The wife may be in a position to work and build up her own pension provision, or she may have other assets which she can use to provide herself with retirement benefits. If she has neither of these options available to her, the aim will be to find sufficient capital for her to invest for that purpose.

6.3.2.1 Use of the *Duxbury* calculation

The conventional method of calculating a lump sum to provide a replacement for maintenance, as used in *Duxbury v Duxbury* [1987] 1 FLR 7, is usually made to provide for the wife throughout her life, both in the immediate future and on retirement. It is a needs-based solution.

In this method, the calculation is based on a number of assumptions including:

(a) the net income required after tax;
(b) the life expectancy of the wife;
(c) the anticipated inflation rate;
(d) the anticipated investment return;
(e) the use of both capital and income so that the wife uses up the entire capital sum during her lifetime.

Many of the larger accountancy firms (and some counsel's chambers) now have the necessary computer programs to carry out the *Duxbury* exercise, although the cost of providing the report can be high. For a rough guide, the *Duxbury* tables produced by the Family Law Bar Association in their publication *At A Glance* (1992) are highly recommended. Where such a calculation is used, and where sufficient capital is available for the husband to pay the lump sum required, there is no need to provide additional capital to compensate for lost retirement benefits, since the capital is designed to provide the necessary income throughout the recipient's life.

Where a woman has no immediate income needs but will need extra income on retirement, a modified calculation could be obtained based on the fact that she needs sufficient capital now to invest to provide an income from, say, age 60 or 65. For a woman who does not need provision until her own retirement, the purchase of an annuity may be the better solution and the calculation of the lump sum can be based on that.

What the wife does with the capital she receives is her own affair, but it may be helpful when calculating the lump sum to take account of how the wife can use the capital, and whether she can invest in her own pension scheme. Whether the wife is able to work or not may make a significant difference to the amount of capital she requires to invest to provide herself with her own provision on retirement.

6.3.2.2 Investment of lump sum in a pension scheme

Wife unable to work

A woman who has no earnings cannot invest her lump sum in her own personal pension scheme because she will have no net relevant earnings. Negotiations to compensate for lost pension rights are all too frequently carried out on the vague suggestion that the wife needs capital 'to invest in a pension scheme'. If she is not working, the capital or investment income (or indeed maintenance) cannot be used in that way. She will have to rely upon more traditional methods of investment which will generally be more expensive (but also more flexible) than investment in her own pension scheme. In these cases, the calculation of the lump sum must be based on anticipated investment performance.

For an older woman, the purchase of an annuity may be the better alternative. The cost of that annuity can be used as the basis for calculating the lump sum to be paid by the husband. This was the method used by

Brandon LJ in a dissenting judgment in *Preston v Preston* (1981) FLR 331 at p 348, where he accepted an argument that an annuity for the wife to yield £30,000 net income for life would cost £310,000, and he based his lump sum calculation on this.

Wife is working or plans to work

A wife with even modest earnings will be able to take out her own personal pension scheme, and because this form of investment is tax efficient it may make a difference to the amount of lump sum she requires, even if only a part of the lump sum is invested in this way. Alternatively, she may be able to make additional voluntary contributions into an occupational pension scheme using all or part of her capital sum.

The maximum percentage earnings which can be invested in a personal pension policy are set out in Chapter 2 at **2.5.5**. For example, a woman aged between 56 and 60 can invest up to 35 per cent of her relevant earnings in this way, and she may be able to invest capital for unused allowances in earlier years. Specialist advice should be sought from a broker about what is the maximum sum she can invest.

Remember that investing in a pension scheme is by no means the only tax efficient type of investment, and it is certainly one of the least flexible.

6.4 DEFERRED COMPENSATION FOR LOSS OF PENSION BENEFITS

An immediate clean break is often too expensive, and adequate compensation may not be available until the husband retires and actually receives his retirement benefit. In these cases, the alternatives are to postpone a decision altogether by having a continuing periodical payments order and adjourned lump sum claim or to have a modified clean break in the form of a deferred lump sum payment. It should be remembered that a husband may be able to opt to take his pension earlier than normal retirement age, and this possibility should be investigated before the decision to postpone is made.

6.4.1 Deferred lump sum order

This solution will be appropriate where the benefits which will be available on retirement are sufficiently clear but no money is available for an immediate clean break. The court has jurisdiction to make an order to pay a lump sum under MCA 1973, s 23(6). There is also jurisdiction under s 23 to pay a lump sum in instalments with the final instalment deferred to a later date such as the husband's retirement date. Precedents for both types of lump sum order are set out in the Appendix, precedents 5 and 6. It should be borne in mind that the deferred instalment(s) must be of a fixed amount. The court cannot in effect make an interim lump sum order by making an order for an initial instalment of the lump sum and then adjourning the balance of the application generally (*Bolsom v Bolsom* (1983) FLR 21 (see, however, *Barry v Barry* [1992] 2 WLR 799)). It is submitted that FPR 1991, r 2.64(2) does not enable a district judge to depart from this principle.

The order can be for a fixed sum or for an amount defined by reference to the level of benefit that will be available to the husband on retirement at a chosen age. It should be noted that a deferred lump sum defined in amount by reference to benefits available to a member of the armed forces will not be possible because of the special statutory provisions relating to them (see **4.8**).

The husband will be able to take only a limited amount of his pension fund as a lump sum. A lump sum equivalent even to the maximum sum which can be taken as a commuted capital payment may therefore be insufficient to meet a wife's pension needs. The maximum amounts which a husband can take under different types of pension scheme have been dealt with in Chapter 2. For example, for personal pension schemes it is fixed at 25 per cent of the fund, for retirement annuity contracts it will be up to roughly 30 per cent, depending on his age at retirement. If the capital sum alone is not enough, a continuing or deferred periodical payments order may be necessary, either in addition to the lump sum or as an alternative.

6.4.1.1 Fixed amount lump sum

A lump sum order for the payment of a fixed amount (for example, where the husband is ordered to pay £50,000 on his attaining the age of 65) will only be suitable if there is a reasonable degree of certainty about the amount which the husband will receive. This type of order was used in *Le Marchant v Le Marchant* [1977] 3 All ER 610, where the husband was ordered to pay a lump sum of £5000 on retirement. A fixed lump sum is not advisable if there is uncertainty about the benefits which the husband will get on retirement.

If the practitioner is acting for the wife, it is important to remember how quickly inflation can eat into an apparently large capital sum. If inflation were at eight per cent per annum over five years, a capital sum of £100,000 payable in five years' time would have an equivalent current value of only £65,908. However, a lump sum order for a fixed amount does have the advantage of certainty and it avoids the necessity of imposing controls over contributions to the pension scheme over the intervening years.

6.4.1.2 Flexible amount lump sum

A lump sum order for the payment of a flexible amount (for example, an order for the husband to pay half the maximum lump sum he can commute on retirement at age 60 from a specified scheme or schemes) was the approach used in *Milne v Milne* (1981) FLR 286. The husband was ordered to pay a lump sum equivalent to half the lump sum he would receive on retirement. The wife also received a periodical payments order.

6.4.1.3 Factors to be taken into account when using deferred lump sum orders

Whether a fixed or flexible deferred lump sum is used, great care must be taken both in predicting the benefits which will be available on retirement and in ensuring that provision is made for any significant intervening events which may occur. For example:

(a) the predictions and calculations must be done either on the basis of the paid up value of the scheme at the time in question with no continuing contributions, or on the basis that continuing contributions of a settled amount are paid. If it is done on the basis of continuing contributions, the husband must undertake to continue to pay at a certain rate until retirement. There can, however, be no control over payments made by employers;

(b) provision must be made to cover the possibility of the husband dying before payment of the deferred lump sum;

(c) provision must be made for the possibility of the husband being forced to retire early due to redundancy or ill-health. This problem may make the fixed lump sum approach unsuitable, since the husband might find himself unable to pay it. The order should be worded to ensure that if the husband does retire earlier than the expected date, the lump sum payment is also brought forward;

(d) it may be a significant disadvantage for the husband to have a deferred order. He might decide to continue working beyond his expected retirement age and yet be forced to take his pension from the date required by the order;

(e) a deferred lump sum order is payable to the wife even if she remarries in the intervening period. If this is not intended, the deferred payment should be conditional upon the wife not remarrying;

(f) a deferred lump sum order survives the death of the wife and can be enforced by the wife's estate. This would not usually be intended and therefore should be specifically excluded;

(g) a lump sum order cannot be varied at a later date if the amount ordered proves insufficient.

6.4.2 Adjournment of applications for a lump sum order

Although adjournments of applications are not popular with the courts, the difficulty of predicting events in the years before retirement gives adjournments many advantages over deferred lump sum orders. As was indicated in Chapter 4 at **4.4**, the courts have traditionally been reluctant to adjourn capital claims but the method will be used as a last resort, where the date on which the husband will retire is not too far in the future.

If adjournment of the application for a lump sum order is contemplated, the following points should be considered.

(a) The husband should be asked to give an undertaking to inform the wife of the date of his retirement or earlier entitlement to benefit under the pension scheme.
(b) Whether the husband should be asked to undertake to make continuing payments to the scheme at a fixed rate.
(c) Provision should be made to cover the wife if the husband dies before the adjourned lump sum claim is revived.
(d) If the wife remarries in the intervening period, she will still technically be able to revive her claim at the appropriate time, unless she is specifically excluded from doing so. Even if her chances of success are diminished by remarriage, her claims may have considerable nuisance value. It may be appropriate for there to be an automatic dismissal of the adjourned lump sum claim on the remarriage of the wife.
(e) Unlike a deferred lump sum order, an adjourned lump sum claim does not survive the death of the wife.
(f) There will be a significant disincentive for the husband to improve his financial position where there is an adjourned claim outstanding, since it may not be limited to a claim against his pension resources. The deferred lump sum payment may therefore be better for both parties.
(g) Adjourning the claim for a lump sum rules out the possibility of an immediate lump sum.

6.4.3 Periodical payments orders

A continuing periodical payments order to compensate for loss of a share in pension benefits has the great advantage of flexibility. If the wife has her own income until she retires, the possibility of a nominal maintenance order with the wife giving an undertaking not to seek an upward variation of that order until her retirement or, in appropriate cases, the husband's retirement, should be considered. The protection given to a wife is even greater where continuing periodical payments are combined with an adjourned lump sum claim or deferred lump sum order to take advantage both of the continuing pension and the commuted lump sum.

In *M v M (Financial Provision)* [1987] 2 FLR 1, a fixed term periodical payments order asked for by the husband was refused on the basis that the wife should have her maintenance claims left open in order to take advantage of the husband's future pension entitlement.

The following points should be borne in mind in relation to periodical payments orders.

(a) The wife will lose her chance of receiving a share of the commuted lump sum if she relies solely on a periodical payments order. Once lump sum claims have been dismissed at the time of the divorce, maintenance can be capitalised into a lump sum only if the husband volunteers such an arrangement (*S v S* [1987] 1 FLR 71).

(b) The wife will lose her entitlement automatically on remarriage or death.

(c) The husband must undertake to inform the wife of the date of retirement or if he decides to take his pension early.

(d) An order for periodical payments, which is expressed to take effect 'until such date as [the wife] shall remarry or until [the husband] retires from [employer] or further order', can be varied only up until one of the specified events occurred (*T v T* [1988] 1 FLR 480). In the circumstances of this unusual case it was held that there was no jurisdiction to entertain an application to vary an order made after the husband retired.

(e) Direct compensation to a wife for lost benefits might be achieved by a husband taking his benefits under a personal pension scheme early (from age 50) and using the extra income to fund periodical payments to her. The husband can take benefits under the scheme and yet continue to work until normal retirement date.

6.5 COMPENSATION FOR LOSS OF DEATH BENEFITS

The previous three sections have dealt with methods of compensation for the general loss of pension benefits, with particular emphasis on the loss of retirement benefits. There are, however, some solutions specific to the loss of benefits which would have been available to the wife on the husband's death had they remained married.

6.5.1 Nominations

Under some statutory and occupational pension schemes, it is possible for the pensioner to give a nomination to the trustees of the pension scheme to take effect in the event of his death. Depending upon the type of scheme, the trustees may then pay to the nominee any death in service benefit, or whatever sum may be available under the death after retirement benefit. However, many schemes will not allow for nominees to be other than a wife or child and in divorce proceedings, this method of ensuring that the wife is protected may therefore be precluded because of the loss of status of the wife. In many schemes, if a wife is nominated as the beneficiary, the nomination is automatically cancelled when the marriage is dissolved. Some schemes allow nominations to separated or former spouses, but the rules of the scheme must be checked.

Another difficulty in practice may arise where trustees have competing claims. Even if a nomination has been made, the trustees are not necessarily bound by that nomination. If, for example, a former wife were given as nominee, and a subsequent wife and child also made a claim to the trustees, the trustees may split the benefits payable, so diluting the benefit to any former wife.

Some nominations are revocable by the pensioner. If no nomination of death in service benefits is made, the lump sum will often fall into the husband's estate and will be distributed in accordance with his will or on intestacy.

Practitioners should give clear written advice about the shortcomings of these arrangements.

A nomination does not have to comply with the formalities of the Wills Act 1837 (*Baird v Baird* [1990] 2 All ER 300).

A nomination form is to be found in the Appendix, precedent 10.

6.5.2 Life assurance

The safest way of compensating a wife for her loss of death benefits will be to arrange for term life assurance to be taken out on the husband's life.

The level of life assurance may be assessed at a lower level than the wife would have received under the pension scheme; indeed, the cost of such arrangements may make this necessary. (For a method of assessing the loss of a widow's rights see [1991] Fam Law 8.) The advice of a reputable broker should be taken on all such matters of investment. In practice, it may be safer to consider the future needs of the recipient, rather than considering the alternative of life assurance as if it were a question purely of compensation.

Some of the different types of policy have been described in Chapter 3. Different types of policy may be appropriate to any particular case, and considerations of cost will usually be paramount. Term assurance will usually be the cheapest option available to produce a lump sum. The term of the policy will usually expire on the husband's anticipated retirement date. However, it is worth considering the convertible type of policy which provides cheap life assurance cover early on but which can later be used for investment purposes.

It may be preferable for the person who has the benefit of the policy to ensure that the premiums are paid by him- or herself. This avoids such problems as the husband giving an undertaking to pay premiums and being bound by that undertaking even after the wife has remarried and is more reliable from the recipient's point of view. However, one should be careful to insure a spouse before decree absolute, because of the rules about insurable interests which are described in more detail in Chapter 3 at **3.2.2**. Failure to do so may not be fatal, because a spouse would continue to have a potential pecuniary loss, but it may lead to difficulties.

It is easy to envisage problems arising where, for example, a husband refuses to have a medical examination. The court has no power to force him to do so. Perhaps the most effective sanction would be to ask for an increased order for maintenance for the amount by which premiums are increased as a result. Perhaps more alarmingly, a particularly difficult husband might deliberately give inaccurate medical evidence or withhold relevant evidence. In such circumstances, because of the strict duty to disclose all material facts to insurers, the company may refuse to honour the terms of the policy. If the proposer's wife were being particularly cautious, she could, no doubt, demand a copy of the relevant part of the proposal form, but even then there is no guarantee that she knows everything about her husband's health.

The case of *Milne v Milne* (1981) 2 FLR 286 has been cited as authority that a court has no power under MCA 1973 to order a spouse to take out a life assurance policy, nor to pay the premiums on such a policy. It is, however, possible under MCA 1973 to order an existing policy to be transferred from one spouse to the other. Similarly, under MCA 1973, s 24(1)(c), it is possible for a court to vary trust provisions, whether under MWPA 1882, s 11 or otherwise.

The assignment of life assurance policies and trust provisions has been considered in Chapter 3.

It may be possible to obtain cheaper insurance through group arrangements; where, for example, a party belongs to the Police Force, special arrangements may apply which would enable a party to obtain similar cover but at much lower rates.

If insurance is not possible, then one might consider the following, each of which is considered in more detail below:

- a contract relating to the husband's will (see **6.5.3**);
- enforcing an order for a lump sum against the estate of the husband (see **6.5.4**); and
- a claim under the Inheritance (Provision for Family and Dependants) Act 1975 (see **6.5.5**).

6.5.3 A contract relating to the a husband's will

Although a will is by its nature always revocable, it is possible for a testator to bind himself personally as to the contents of his will. An agreement to this effect would ensure that his personal representatives, whether he dies testate or intestate, must give effect to that agreement at the expense of the beneficiaries under his will or intestacy. For it to be effective, there has to be a binding agreement by the testator to dispose of his property in a certain way. This agreement must satisfy two certainties:

(1) certainty of subject matter – the description of the property or legacy must not be too vague, the freehold or leasehold property must be specified or the precise sum must be given;
(2) certainty of obligation – there must either be a binding contract, or an agreement by deed.

Care must be taken to ensure that the covenant or agreement is not rendered unenforceable by reason of non-compliance with the Law of Property (Miscellaneous Provisions) Act 1989, s 2. Therefore, if a contract other than a deed of covenant relates to land, it must be in writing. See generally, *Williams on Wills* 6th edn (Butterworths, 1987) Ch 2.

On divorce, if a husband contracts to devise or bequeath specific property, then the agreement is enforceable by way of damages for its breach and the remedy by way of damages may be claimed immediately the husband puts it out of his power to perform this obligation, even while he is alive. The wife can intervene before a purchaser for value without notice obtains an interest in the property, and she can register the contract or a caution against the title (see *Schaefer v Schuhmann* [1972] 1 All ER 621).

If the agreement does not deal with specific land, for example if the husband contracts to leave a share of money of which he may die possessed, the danger is that he will be at liberty to spend or dispose of all or any of this money during his life. However, if money is spent on land, then that land is charged with a sum equal to the purchase money in favour of the covenantee. Further, the covenantee's claim cannot be defeated by testamentary disposition.

Apart from prior disposition of non-specific property, another problem arises because of the Inheritance (Provision for Family and Dependants) Act 1975, s 25: this provides that the 'net estate' can be deemed for the purposes of the Act, to include property which is the subject of a contract of this type. This means that the contract can be effectively overridden by an order under that Act.

It is also possible for a covenant to be made not to revoke a will or a particular clause in a will. Whilst this would prevent revocation by the husband, it would not prevent revocation by operation of law, for example if the husband remarried, or on lapse. None the less, despite the obvious shortcomings of this procedure, it may be of help to the practitioner in ensuring that a wife has some provision on the death of a husband or former husband, without any immediate expense necessarily being incurred.

6.5.4 Enforcement of orders against the estate of a party

An order for unsecured periodical payments will not survive the death of the person against whom it was made. This is not the case where there is an order for secured periodical payments.

In the case of lump sum or property adjustment orders, the order survives the death of the person against whom it is made and the order can be enforced by or against his estate (see eg *Warren-Gash and Another v Lane* [1984] Fam Law 184). If the death of one party falls soon after the order is made, then an appeal may be appropriate. One should consider in particular the guidelines set out in the case of *Barder v Barder (Caluori Intervening)* [1987] 2 FLR 480.

6.5.5 Claims under the Inheritance (Provision for Family and Dependants) Act 1975

A claim under the Inheritance (Provision for Family and Dependants) Act 1975 is something of a last resort, and should always be considered as such. When acting for the wife, and where there is no possible other means of compensating her for the loss of death benefit or widow's pension to provide for her needs on the death of the former husband, then it may be necessary to consider a claim under this Act. It is important to ensure that such a claim remains open.

There are a number of practical disadvantages to relying upon a claim under this Act.

(a) A claim is possible only if the husband dies domiciled in England and Wales.
(b) Despite the provisions enabling the avoidance of disposition, the claim is still dependent upon what is in the net estate.
(c) There may well be other dependants whose claims have to be balanced against those of a former wife.

CHAPTER 7

LEGAL FRAMEWORK: DRAFTING AND ENFORCEMENT

7.1 INTRODUCTION

Much useful time and expense may have been spent upon identifying the pension benefits available to the parties, valuing those benefits, and arriving at the most appropriate solution to compensate for the loss. If, however, the terms reached between the parties are not incorporated into a form of agreement which is enforceable in the event of non-compliance, that time and expense may be thrown away and may leave the practitioner open to a negligence claim.

7.2 DRAFTING

The practitioner's skill is particularly required in drafting consent orders to ensure that the order both accurately reflects the terms of the agreement reached between the parties and that it will prove enforceable in the event of non-compliance. The words of Lord Oliver of Aylmerton in *Dinch v Dinch* [1987] 2 FLR 162 at p 164 deserve careful consideration:

> 'It is in all cases the imperative professional duty of those invested with the task of advising the parties to these unfortunate disputes to consider with due care the impact which any terms which they agree on behalf of their clients has, and is intended to have, upon any outstanding application for ancillary relief, and to ensure that such appropriate provision is inserted in any consent order made as will leave no room for any future doubt or misunderstanding, or saddle the parties with the wasteful burden of wholly unnecessary costs.'

When drafting a consent order, there are two important questions to be considered:

- is it within the jurisdiction of the court? If so, it can be an order of the court; if not, it should be dealt with by way of an undertaking (see *Livesey (Formerly Jenkins) v Jenkins* [1985] FLR 813 at p 829; and
- how will the obligation be enforced? This issue is addressed at **7.3** et seq.

Consent orders generally fall into four constituent parts:

– recitals (which provide a narrative or historic introduction) – agreements – undertakings	Preamble to the order
– orders	Operative part of the order

Although the lack of an introductory recital will not in any way invalidate the order, the inclusion of such a recital may be an aid to construction if there is some later ambiguity in the operative part of the order.

Matters which may not be dealt with in the operative part of the order because the court does not have power to make an order in such terms, frequently those relating to pension provision, should be dealt with by way of agreement or undertaking. There is, however, no need for agreements or undertakings to duplicate matters referred to in the operative part of the order.

As a general rule, an undertaking should be used when either party is under an obligation to perform a specific act, or series of acts, whereas actions which have already been carried out, or which are to be carried out jointly by the parties, will be reflected as an agreement between them. There are, however, some exceptions to this general rule. For example, there is no purpose in incorporating in an order an undertaking which will have the effect of ousting the jurisdiction of the court's own jurisdiction, since such an undertaking will not be enforceable and should not be accepted by the court. If, however, the agreed terms were dealt with by means of a recited agreement, it may still be of dubious enforceability but will be of some evidential value to which the court might have regard as a matter of conduct under MCA 1973, ss 25 and 31(7).

Although it is hoped that the precedents in the Appendix will be of assistance to the practitioner, they are intended as specimens only. Anyone using them in whole or in part should determine their appropriateness and adapt them as may be required to fit the particular circumstances of each case.

There are a number of reasons why drafting an order which incorporates provision for loss of pension benefits may require particular care. First, the agreement reached between the parties may contain a provision which the practitioner does not encounter on a regular basis and for which he does not have available a tried and trusted precedent. Secondly, not only must the practitioner be alert to whether what he is trying to do is within the jurisdiction of the court, he must also consider whether the action which one party has agreed to take is within his power to carry into effect, as is seen below.

7.3 ENFORCEMENT

If the solution which has been arrived at provides for payment of a quantified or easily quantifiable lump sum, the drafting of the order should be a relatively straightforward task. The practitioner generally has to ensure only that the date for payment of the lump sum is specified, and that that date is after pronouncement of the final decree. Additionally, where appropriate, the payment of interest should be specifically provided if it has been agreed that interest should be payable prior to the date when payment of the lump sum is due. However, it is not necessary to provide specifically for interest to be payable *after* the date when the lump sum is due, as such interest is payable automatically either in the High Court (Judgments Act 1838) or the county court (County Courts (Interest on Judgment Debts) Order 1991) providing in the latter case the order was made on or after 1 July 1991 and is for £5000 or more. In cases where a more complex solution has been arrived at, the following considerations should be borne in mind when drafting the wording of the order to ensure that the agreement is capable of enforcement.

7.3.1 Is it possible for an agreed course of action to be taken?

There is little or no value in arriving at a solution which involves one party in agreeing to take a step which it is not within his power to carry out. For example, if one party does not have an insurable interest in the other's life, it will not be possible for an insurance policy to be taken out upon that person's life, even if both parties wish to do so. In that event, the problem may be solved by the person whose life is to be assured taking out an appropriate policy and assigning the benefit of the policy to the intended beneficiary – this is frequently an appropriate solution where a wife no longer has an insurable interest in her former husband's life because the decree nisi has already been made absolute. Similarly, a member of a pension scheme cannot bind the trustees to pay the death-in-service benefit or any other benefits arising under his pension to a third party, even if it has been agreed by the husband and wife that this would be the most appropriate course of action to take. Indeed, if the husband attempts to bind the trustees to pay such benefits to a third party, this may have the undesirable effect of rendering him and his former wife ineligible to receive any benefits under the scheme because of the effect of a spendthrift clause of the type which is invariably contained in pension schemes. A similar result will ensue where a wife attempts to enforce a maintenance order against a pension already in payment, for example by means of an attachment of earnings order (*Edmonds v Edmonds* [1965] 1 All ER 379).

A distinction can, however, be made between an undertaking to make an irrevocable nomination of the death-in-service benefit, and the trustees being bound by such a nomination. If the husband's nomination is expressed to be irrevocable, this will provide further evidence of the intention of the parties, which may have a greater influence upon the trustees, but will still not be binding upon them. However, if the trustees do not follow the nomination, the undertaking will remain enforceable against the husband's estate.

Where an agreement would involve a third party taking a step which he has a discretion to do, but which he cannot be forced to take, it is important to ensure that an alternative method of securing provision is available to the payee if the third party does not exercise his discretion in the manner envisaged (cf *G v G (Financial Provision: Discovery)* [1992] 1 FLR 40). Nominations for receipt of death-in-service benefits or benefits which are payable upon death after retirement, such as a widow's pension, can be a minefield. If the pension trustees choose not to be bound by a valid nomination made by a husband in favour of his former wife in respect of his death-in-service benefit, she may be without the means to secure alternative provision, particularly if her claims under the Inheritance (Provision for Family and Dependants) Act 1975 have been excluded. Agreement to the exclusion of such claims is justified therefore only if it is absolutely certain that payments which it is agreed are to be made in the future will in fact be made, or where there is a procedure in place which can be used to enforce such payment, such as where the husband is making secured periodical payments. Even where claims under the Inheritance (Provision for Family and Dependants) Act 1975 have not been excluded, there is no guarantee that the deceased's estate will be sufficient to merit such a claim, or that such a claim will succeed. Such a claim should be viewed only as a last resort and not as a guaranteed means for ensuring that financial provision will be available in the future.

7.3.2 Ensuring that agreed steps have been taken

Provision should be made in the order to enable the payee to verify that the payer has taken all agreed steps. For example, if the wife finds out after the death of her husband that he has failed to make an agreed nomination in respect of his death-in-service benefits and he has died leaving a dependant cohabitee and young children, it is too late to take any remedial action. If approached directly, the pension trustees will usually refuse to disclose whether such a nomination has been made and the husband should therefore give an undertaking to make the nomination within a specified time and provide evidence that the nomination has been made in the agreed terms and received by the pension trustees (see Appendix, precedent 10).

Where the agreement involves a continuing course of action, provision should be made to verify its continuance. For example, if a life insurance policy is to be taken out by the payer, it may be possible for him to give his authority for the payee to be notified by the insurance company direct if the premiums are not paid, or for the insurance company to be given an authority to provide such information relating to the policy as the payee may from time to time request (see Appendix, precedent 3(b)). This particular problem will not arise if the policy is taken out by the payee on the payer's life.

The situation is more difficult to control if it is open to the life insured to take steps in the future which would have the effect of preventing the intended beneficiary from receiving an agreed payment, but which could be taken without the beneficiary's knowledge. For example, an insurance policy may exclude payment where the life insured undertakes a dangerous activity. If the life insured's death resulted from engaging in such an activity, the beneficiary may have no source of recompense, even if the life insured had undertaken not to become involved in such an activity, or not to do anything which may invalidate or prejudice the policy. It may be possible to take proceedings against the insured's estate in the event of breach of the undertaking not to invalidate the policy causing the death of the insured, or in the event of breach of an undertaking to provide life cover. However, such proceedings would not be justified if there are not sufficient assets in the estate. Where the time of discovery that an undertaking has been breached renders it impossible to enforce the undertaking, the fact that such an undertaking was given may assist if alternative provision is sought, for example under the Inheritance (Provision for Family and Dependants) Act 1975. Similarly, pension scheme trustees may be more inclined to make provision for a member's former wife if it can be shown that that member breached an undertaking given by him to provide his former wife with other means of financial support.

Where the practitioner is aware that an agreement has shortcomings, such as the possibility of pension trustees declining to accept nominations of death-in-service benefits, clear written advice should be given to the client concerning the matter. This will therefore give the client the opportunity to decide whether a more certain form of financial provision should be sought, even if such provision would be for a smaller amount.

7.3.3 What enforcement procedures are available?

Apart from payment of money by one party to the proceedings to the other party, the only other likely form of provision for loss of pension benefit which may be incorporated into the body of the order is an assignment of a life insurance policy (which the court has power to order as a property adjustment order). Most of the other solutions considered in Chapter 6 will need to be provided for by way of agreement or undertaking. In *Livesey* above, Lord Brandon discussed how obligations under an agreement which do not come within the court's powers under ss 23 and 24 of the Matrimonial Causes Act 1973 should be incorporated into a consent order:

> '. . . the proper procedure for incorporating the obligations concerned into a consent order is by formulating them as undertakings given to the Court. Such undertakings are, needless to say, enforceable as effectively as direct orders.'

In order to ensure that the undertaking is enforceable, its wording must make clear what steps are to be taken and within what time limit. It will then generally be open to the recipient of the undertaking to take enforcement proceedings in the event of non-compliance with the undertaking.

If enforcement of the undertaking is to be by way of, for example charging order, execution or garnishee, it is not necessary to convert the undertaking (assuming this is possible) into an order before enforcement because an undertaking given to the court and embodied in a written order has the same effect as an order in the terms of the undertaking (*Gandolfo v Gandolfo* [1980] 1 All ER 833). However, if an undertaking has been given to make payments of a sum or sums of money, its breach may not be enforceable by means of committal. Under s 11 of the Administration of Justice Act 1970, the power of committal under the Debtors Act 1869 is limited to enforcement of maintenance, income tax and certain social security premiums and contributions. 'Maintenance' is defined in s 28(1) and Sch 8 to the Administration of Justice Act 1970 (as amended) as being an order for periodical payments or other payments made, or having effect as if made, under Part II of the Matrimonial Causes Act 1973. This, therefore, would appear to include a lump sum order as well as an order for periodical payments. Undertakings to pay insurance premiums and other similar provisions which are likely to have been agreed as compensation for loss of pension benefits may be enforceable by committal. Such undertakings cannot be asserted as a contempt of court warranting imprisonment because of the basic prohibition in the 1869 Act. However, different considerations will apply if the undertaking is treated as falling within the preserved classes of debt enforceable by judgment summons (see [1992] Fam Law 233).

Where committal is available, it is imperative that the committal procedure is strictly adhered to. There is a substantial body of case law in which errors in the committal procedure, even those of a minor nature, have rendered the procedure void (see *Re M (Minors) (Access: Contempt: Committal)* [1991] 1 FLR 355 and *Lewis v Lewis* [1991] Fam Law 469).

7.4 CONCLUSION

It is hoped that this chapter has gone some way towards identifying the considerations which must be foremost in the draftsman's mind. The need to ensure that the wording of the order accurately reflects the terms of the agreement reached, and will prove to be enforceable in the event of non-compliance, cannot be over-emphasised. A systematic approach, together with time and care spent upon the drafting of the order, will produce their own reward if only in alleviating the frustration (not to mention expense) of discovering that the consent order does not say what it was thought to have said.

CHAPTER 8

LEGAL FRAMEWORK: PROPOSALS FOR REFORM AND THE INTERNATIONAL SCENE

8.1 PROPOSALS FOR REFORM

8.1.1 Introduction

The search for a fair and practical system for dividing pension rights between divorcing spouses has gone on for many years. That such a system is desirable has long been accepted, but how it should and could be achieved remains unresolved.

The difficulties are easy to see. The whole issue has to be viewed within the context of the law relating to ancillary relief as a whole rather than as an isolated problem. Arrangements for the division of pension rights will only be part of a wider agreement or court order, dealing with maintenance, capital and property claims. The English legal system has placed considerable emphasis on the court's powers to exercise its discretion in each individual case and, therefore, treating any one aspect of ancillary relief in a significantly different way by imposing a formula will be difficult.

Discretion, it is argued, gives the court the greatest opportunity to do justice in any particular set of circumstances. However, it is also argued that the lack of any clear guidelines makes a settlement more difficult to reach, and orders more difficult to predict, thus encouraging litigation and wasting costs. This dilemma applies to pensions as much as to ancillary matters generally. Pensions are by their very nature, however, significantly different from any of the other assets which have to be dealt with. Whilst the value will often be substantial, it is not freely available to either party, nor is it within the power of the court to free the money. In addition, it is not possible to predict with total accuracy what the asset will be worth at the time that it becomes available to a party, nor is it possible to know what the parties' circumstances will be at the time the asset becomes available.

The English court has never favoured a mathematical approach to resolving ancillary relief claims, and such attempts as there have been to introduce formulae (for example, the 'one-third rule') have been restricted. There is almost always a reason for a court to distinguish a case 'on its own facts' where it does not want to follow precedent. Statute has given the court a wide discretion which it shows no sign of wishing to relinquish. However, signs of a change in this attitude were evidenced by the Government's White Paper *Children Come First* (Cm 1263, 2 vols) which led, in turn, to the Child Support Act 1991 and the setting up of the Child Support Agency. Under the

Act, most child maintenance will be calculated by reference to a standard formula, and the discretion of the court will be significantly diminished. The arguments raised for and against such an approach are in many ways similar to those raised in the pensions debate, although with pensions the problems are more complex.

There are five interested groups who will be affected by any proposed change in the way that pensions are treated on divorce. The first two, the divorcing spouses, will usually have quite contrary interests. The husband may remarry and wish his pension to benefit his new wife and family. The divorced wife on the other hand will wish to benefit as fully as she can and to be placed as closely as possible to the position in which she would have been had she remained married; this would mean not only preserving her eligibility for the widow's pension, but also enabling her to benefit from the pension payments themselves as soon as they are available to the husband.

Also interested however is the third group, the pensions industry itself; those who administer and provide the various forms of pension schemes. Their interest is to provide the most attractive form of pension possible to the customer, and the customer is usually the husband. In the majority of cases, therefore, their interests will be his interests. In addition, however, they will also bear the burden of increased administration in calculating the benefits due to former spouses and keeping records of such entitlement which may result from any new system. This is not something which they are likely to welcome.

The fourth interested party is made up of the dependants of the husband, most importantly his children. Although, in theory, the court has the same power on divorce to make lump sum orders for the children as it does for the wife, that power is rarely exercised. In practice, the lump sum and property adjustment orders made in respect of the wife will also have to satisfy the needs of any dependants living with her. It is, of course, possible that the children may be of an age when they are no longer living at home, in which case they may have a contrary interest to that of the wife. The husband may prefer to benefit his children rather than his wife, and therefore any claim that she is able to make may diminish what they would otherwise receive.

The fifth interested party is the State, which may have to bear the burden of providing for any former wife who is not sufficiently provided for by her former husband.

8.1.2 Law Commission proposals

The first significant examination of the pension problem was carried out by the Law Commission in its *Report on Financial Provision in Matrimonial Proceedings* in 1969. Having identified the potential hardships for divorced wives and the problems of devising a satisfactory solution, the report was unable to provide any answers, commenting only that other statutory provisions and State benefits should offset any hardship resulting from this problem.

In 1980 the Law Commission returned to the problem in its discussion paper *The Financial Consequences of Divorce: The Basic Policy* (1980 Cmnd 8041). This expanded further upon the problems but made limited proposals for legislation to enable the courts to deal with occupational pensions. These applied only in the cases of older women or those whose responsibilities to children effectively precluded them from having the opportunity of earning their own pension. When the Matrimonial and Family Proceedings Act 1984 implemented recommendations in the report, it did not deal with the proposed provisions dealing with pensions. It was felt that this area was a problem which required more thought and discussion before any changes were made to the existing law. (See also **8.1.5**.)

8.1.3 Occupational Pensions Board Proposals

The Occupational Pensions Board (OPB) produced its proposals in 1975. In *Equal Status For Men and Women in Occupational Pension Schemes* (1975 Cmnd 6599), the OPB proposed that the court should have jurisdiction in appropriate cases to order that a former wife should receive part or all of pension rights which, under the scheme, would be payable to a widow. This should also apply to the guaranteed minimum pension.

This proposal is unattractive to husbands, because they will lose part of what they will see as their asset, and particularly as it is an asset to which they may continue to contribute long after divorce. The effect of the proposal is also to deprive any future wife of a husband and, indeed, any future family, of part or even all of the entitlement which they would have otherwise received, even though the second marriage may eventually subsist longer than the first.

From the former wife's point of view, the proposal is unsatisfactory in that, whilst she may receive some compensation for loss of a share in pension benefits in due course, it will not be payable until the death of the former husband. If there has otherwise been a clean break, and her rights to maintenance have been terminated, her former husband may enjoy his pension for a considerable number of years without her being able to make any claim on it.

The proposal also places the court in an invidious position. A husband who divorces in his late thirties could quite conceivably have one or more further wives, and families, or he may never remarry at all. None the less, the court at the time of the divorce would have to make an order capable of doing justice to all concerned. In addition, such orders would offend against the 'clean break' principle.

The OPB also, and perhaps somewhat optimistically, recommended that those providing pensions should adopt more flexible rules in relation to the allocation of pension benefits between different beneficiaries. It is difficult to see what incentive there could be for this: the pension industry would thereby make its own task of administration more complicated and expensive, whilst offering what, in most circumstances, would be seen by the customer as a less desirable product.

8.1.4 Lord Chancellor's Department paper

The Lord Chancellor's Department (LCD) produced a consultation paper in July 1985 *Occupational Pension Rights on Divorce*. The paper limited its considerations to widow's pensions, although reference was made to the wider question of dividing pension rights as a whole, not simply upon the husband's death. The LCD paper, like that of the Law Commission before it in 1980, considered provision of only a limited class, namely those with young children, and older women, and only then when it could be shown that, in the absence of special provision, there would be hardship. In keeping with the principle of allowing the court to exercise its discretion on the facts of each case, a two-stage approach was recommended. It proposed that a claim should, at the court's discretion, be registered at the time of divorce, but not adjudicated on until the death of the former husband. This had the advantage that it would allow the court the opportunity to consider the circumstances as they existed on the former husband's death, but had the great disadvantage of effectively prolonging the ancillary relief proceedings throughout the joint lives of the parties. Quite apart from this, such a proposal would be highly unpopular with the pension industry, and might have a considerable effect on the cost of providing any pension which included provision for widows. If the husband may be deemed in law to have left a 'widow', even if he has divorced, the number of potential claimants will inevitably be much greater. Consequently, greater contributions would be required in order to meet the increased number of claims. The proposal also ignores the fact that the person who then has to suffer financially is not the former husband, who will enjoy his full pension during his lifetime, but any subsequent wife who survives him.

8.1.5 Proposals of the Institute for Fiscal Studies

In 1988, the Institute for Fiscal Studies proposed a different approach in their report *Property and Marriage: An Integrated Approach* ((1988) IFS Report 29). The report, as its title suggests, looked at the question of matrimonial property in its entirety, and suggested that, if the present system did not produce what was considered to be a fair result, then the solution was to change the whole system rather than attempting to correct its faults by adding further detail.

The main proposal was to follow an approach similar to that used in many other countries where there is 'community of property'. Some of these foreign schemes are referred to briefly below. Typically, the assets of the spouses are valued and, after making allowances for the assets which each of them brought into the marriage and for certain other assets, such as those received by way of gift or inheritance, the balance is divided between them according to set rules. The IFS report proposed that pension rights accruing during the marriage should be treated as an asset and, on divorce, half the assets, including the pension rights, which had accrued during the marriage, should belong to the wife. She would then be treated either as a separate member of the husband's scheme or could take the transfer value of her share into her own pension.

While this proposal runs contrary to the 'clean break' principle (although it is difficult to see how any scheme, except where there are very large assets, can do otherwise), it does at least start to overcome the various deficiencies of the earlier reports. It provides a basis for calculating what the former wife will gain, and what the husband will lose, and by fixing the entitlement at the time of divorce it avoids further litigation at some indefinite point in the future. The former wife will also be able to enjoy the benefits under the pension when it falls due (as would have been the case if she had remained married) rather than having to await the former husband's death.

Interestingly, later that same year the Law Commission took a different view on community of property. *Family Law – Matrimonial Property* (Law Com No 175) looked at property ownership in marriage, but not specifically in relation to divorce. The question of pensions was not specifically addressed in the report. Part 3 of the report deals with the possible approaches to reform. At 3.3, the report acknowledges the enthusiasm in some circles for 'the wholesale introduction of community of property during marriage'. It acknowledged that the proposal was of sufficient merit to justify detailed consideration, but still went on to reject it. The report found that countries with a completely separate system of property had moved towards partial or deferred community. However, where this meant equal division on divorce, with little discretion to reallocate, the system was considered unsatisfactory, suggesting that more discretion was required. This, in turn, created a complexity which was considered undesirable and unlikely to be acceptable in practice.

8.1.6 Labour party policy: the Meacher scheme

The general principle of the IFS proposal was taken up by the Labour MP Michael Meacher when he produced a consultation paper entitled *Pensions, Couples and Divorce* in May 1990. Whilst not claiming to provide a solution to all the problems involved, the paper states that it is intended to ensure that men and women alike, whether married or cohabiting, receive a fair share of the pension assets accrued during the period of their relationship. It proposes that spouses should be able to register their interest in their partner's pensions, and it suggests that this should be automatic for married couples and available as a right to cohabitees on request. Where an interest is registered, each partner would have the right to a half share of the pension's value on the community of property principle. On divorce, or separation in the case of cohabitees, the assets would be valued and split equally. The paper also acknowledges the problems posed by the different types of pension provision available. Among its other recommendations, it acknowledges the need to give the court power to order pension benefits to be divided, whilst allowing the parties to come to their own arrangements by agreement. It recognises the need for legislation to facilitate the smooth operation of the scheme.

The Meacher scheme received a qualified welcome, but was still criticised within the pension industry as being complicated and too inflexible. Central to the effective implementation of the proposal would be an accurate calculation of transfer values, which is, in itself, a complicated matter involving considerable administrative costs.

8.1.7 The Law Society

In May 1991, the Family Law Committee of the Law Society published *Maintenance and Capital Provision on Divorce* which, at p 17, included a section on the issue of pension-splitting. The report very succinctly sets out the various pension-related benefits which a court will have to consider and the problems which the courts have experienced in trying to deal with pensions under the existing law. The Committee considered that the proposals of the Law Commission and the Lord Chancellor's Department were unsatisfactory, but viewed with more favour the proposals from the IFS and Michael Meacher. The Committee, however, highlighted that the proposals failed to take account of the limited existing powers of the courts to deal with pension-splitting. The report concluded that 'if consistency is to be achieved in arrangements for pension-splitting on divorce, it can only be done by way of primary legislation. The Committee thinks that this legislation should provide that the courts have the power to make a pension adjustment order at the time of the ancillary relief hearing.' The Committee went on to recommend that the courts should be given power to make pension adjustment orders in proceedings under the Matrimonial Causes Act 1973, and should be provided with powers similar to those available under the Scottish legislation (see **8.2.1**), and that there should be a power to allow payments by a former husband into a personal pension scheme for a wife. Guidance should be issued on how and when a pension should be valued, and in what shares it should be split.

In its conclusions, the Committee states that reform in this area of law was long overdue and that 'it is essential to ensure that a coherent and consistent system is produced which will ensure that wives receive some benefit from pension rights accrued by their husbands during the marriage'.

Whilst the Committee leaves the detail of its recommendations to be refined, its paper indicates the growing awareness of the problem among family lawyers and of the need for substantive reform.

8.1.8 The Pensions Management Institute

In September 1991, the Pensions Management Institute (PMI) published *Pensions and Divorce* by Robin Ellison, one of the country's foremost pension lawyers. The report draws upon a wealth of research and discussion on the issues of pension-splitting both in this country and abroad. It is a valuable contribution to the debate, as previously the problem had been addressed by people who were not generally pension experts. Any change will rely heavily upon the pensions industry itself to implement it and, therefore, for any scheme to be truly effective it must meet the concerns of the pension providers.

The report suggests that:

> 'whatever is recommended, the recommendation needs to bear in mind the following requirements:
> - The need for equity, though not a chimerical absolute equity;
> - The need for simplicity, both in calculation and administration, to avoid muddling the Courts and parties;
> - The need for a nil cost on pension schemes, to avoid employers and monogamous members subsidising serially polygamous members;
> - Conformity with the clean break requirements of modern divorce law, to avoid clogging the system of judicial administration.
>
> Whatever scheme is introduced, there will be anomalies, paradoxes and inequities. Provided they are not excessive, they may well be acceptable.'

Although, as the book itself has clearly stated, it is written from the point of view of the pension provider, it seems difficult to fault this synopsis generally. Obviously, the need for some basic standard of fairness is paramount, and if at all possible it would be advisable to avoid the complexity of some of the foreign schemes (see, for example, West Germany, at **8.2.3**). If the pensions industry is to give effect to any scheme, costs need to be kept as low as possible. It must be borne in mind that there will be a number of contributors to pensions who will not be affected and who should not therefore be expected to bear unduly increased costs. Whilst it would be desirable to keep as closely as possible within the clean break principle, Ellison does acknowledge that:

> 'it may be that with all the other problems of enforcement that might arise, pensions should be considered a special issue, and should be exempted from the normal clean break principles.'

In trying to meet the main requirements, the questions of quantum and allocation are highlighted.

> 'The question of quantum is one which few of the jurisdictions seem satisfactorily to have tackled. In practice, there always seem to be problems with the valuation of pension rights that are split – whether they should take account of future salary growth, future additional accruals and a future assets performance.'

Clearly, no solution is going to be ideal, and a balance needs to be struck between the competing needs of fairness, simplicity and low cost.

Allocation would ideally be settled at the time of the divorce, in order to meet the clean break objective. The report recommends that wherever possible the pension is taken into account as one of the assets, but that it is the other, more readily available, assets which are adjusted to take account of the pension. In practice, however, this is unlikely to be workable except in high asset cases. It therefore proposes that the second option should be to make an order for 'deferred maintenance' against a spouse, rather than against the pension fund and contingent survivor's pensions should then be registrable in the land charges registry. Pension fund trustees should be under an obligation to check the register before paying the member's benefit. Pension-splitting should only be adopted as a last resort where no other solution is possible, in which case there would have to be a fundamental change in several areas of the law.

The PMI report, overall, presents a very clear outline of the issues and some highly constructive comments on some of the possible answers, whilst acknowledging that there is more work to be done. Indeed, as stated on p 48:

> 'the remainder of this Paper is intended as a discussion document, rather than a statement of complete solution. Its function is to promote comment and thought about a problem that is likely to increase. It is hoped that out of the response to this and other Papers, a practical answer can emerge.'

That wish will no doubt be echoed by all concerned with this question. The Report is written 'more from the viewpoint of the pensions provider, than from the viewpoint of the divorce industry'. Its proposals may not find total favour with family lawyers because of the suggested inroad into the clean break principle based upon treatment of pension expectations as 'deferred maintenance' rather than as an asset in their own right.

8.1.9 Conclusion

These are far from being the only views and proposals which have been put forward (see William Goodhart, 'Occupational Pension Schemes in Divorce – a new proposal' *Trust Law and Practice* April 1988 and Dr Judith Masson, 'Pensions Dependency and Divorce' *Journal of Social Welfare Law*, 1986). One can discern the competing claims of clean break, treasured by family lawyers, and the pensions industry which is reluctant for administrative reasons to call for substantive change to pension schemes which were designed when the nuclear family was the norm. It remains to be seen whether the Government will feel that any solution of sufficient certainty and practicability has emerged to merit statutory backing.

8.2 OTHER JURISDICTIONS

Having considered at some length the history of the deliberations in this country as to how to deal with pensions on family breakdown, it is instructive to look abroad to see how other jurisdictions have dealt with the problem. Some jurisdictions have a radically different approach to pensions, largely because their approach to divorce proceedings, in general, is different. Even within the British Isles there are other approaches: the law of Scotland already includes some specific provision for dealing with pensions.

8.2.1 Scotland

The relevant law is contained in the Family Law (Scotland) Act 1985 (FLSA 1985). This amended the broad discretion conferred on the courts by the

Divorce (Scotland) Act 1976. FLSA 1985 made specific provision under s 10(5) that occupational pension schemes and life policies are to be included in the definition of 'matrimonial property'. Section 9(1) provided that 'the net value of the matrimonial property should be shared fairly between the parties to the marriage'. 'Fairly' is equally, unless special circumstances apply. No provision is made as to how a pension or life policy is to be valued. Life policies have a surrender value which can be used, but for pensions an actuarial valuation is often required. As there is no fixed basis for valuation, actuaries can, and do, adopt different approaches.

A Scottish court has no greater powers than an English court to reallocate pension rights and benefits between the spouses and therefore its powers, in practice, may be severely limited. Unless the pension benefits are already available, any adjustment can only be indirect, by making provision from other resources to compensate, or by creating deferred rights. This system does not seem to have been particularly successful and there is no shortage of criticism.

In 'Pensions Rights on Divorce: Clean Breaks or Dirty Breaks?' (*Journal of the Law Society of Scotland*, Feb 1991) R Andrew Scott FFA, an actuary, sets out a detailed criticism, with examples, and suggests that whilst FLSA 1985 is a step in the right direction, it gives no guidance as to the basis of valuation and then requires the pension 'owner' to make payment now, by adjustment of other assets, for a benefit he has not yet received and, indeed, may never receive if he dies in service. Scott concludes by noting that 'Most, if not all, of the people I talked to expressed dissatisfaction with the current practice'. More damningly '. . . my recommendation for any Scot contemplating divorce is to move to England first!'.

8.2.2 Canada: Alberta

The Institute of Law Research and Reform of Edmonton, Alberta, Canada produced a report in 1985 called *Matrimonial Property: Division of Pension Benefits upon Marriage Breakdown* (Report No 48). The stated aim of the report is to achieve fairness between spouses, to avoid or minimise the future entanglement of their financial affairs, to facilitate and encourage settlements, to minimise the financial and emotional costs of the division of the property, and to protect the interests of employers, other employees and pension plans and funds.

The report takes the view that spouses have an interest in benefits which have accumulated up to the time of division of the matrimonial property. The report therefore recommends against the sharing of increases in a pension benefit accruing after division. Such increases would include pension increases resulting from increased salaries under a final earnings plan.

The report recommends that a variety of methods for dividing pension benefits should be employed. Already available under their jurisdiction are 'valuation and accounting', whereby the husband pays the wife for the wife's assessed share of the pension benefit, and 'division of proceeds', whereby the husband or the pension plan pays the wife an assessed share from

such difference. Where the parties have similar types of pension, the court has powers to transfer part of one party's entitlement to the other party's scheme so as to produce a balance, but where there are differing types of scheme there are extensive powers to allocate part of one pension scheme for the benefit of the other spouse. It is interesting to note that the scheme, although comprehensive, has itself run into a number of problems because some of its provisions have, from time to time, been declared unconstitutional. It must be inevitable that a complex scheme, where no discretion is permitted, will create some situations which are not at all what was intended.

The German scheme applies almost automatically, and it is very difficult to 'contract out' of it. There does not have to be a specific application for division of pensions, a division follows in almost all cases where there is a divorce.

8.2.4.2 Austria

The Austrian system is rather different, but also starts from quite a different premise. (It might be considered that in some ways the Austrian system is less advanced than the UK's, as in certain circumstances the financial provision is dependent on whether or not the party seeking relief was adjudged to be at fault in respect of the divorce itself.) The basic premise is that parties maintain separate ownership of property during divorce, each owns the assets which they brought into the marriage, and those assets they acquire during the marriage. On divorce, the law first requires the parties to attempt to divide their property by mutual consent. In the absence of any such agreement the court decides, although even then certain assets, for example those received by way of inheritance or gift, are exempted from these claims. The court distinguishes between property and household goods, and savings.

Entitlement to maintenance can be affected by a party's conduct in bringing about the breakdown of the marriage, but subject to this, pension rights are taken into account in calculating what each party should receive. The court, however, does not have powers to directly apportion the pension but can give a spouse rights to be maintained after the death of the pension-owning spouse. The amount of a 'pension claim' is limited by the amount of maintenance to which it is adjudged the spouse is entitled.

8.3 CONCLUSION

No country appears to have yet developed a system which deals with pensions on divorce in a way which is satisfactory to the legal practitioners of that country. It seems unlikely that such a system is possible. Each State has to decide on the balance of complexity and certainty, cost and flexibility, which seems to suit it best, and this balance will almost certainly change with time, particularly as economic and social circumstances alter the financial relationships between spouses.

GLOSSARY

This glossary includes the technical terms generally used in relation to pensions and life assurance and referred to in this book. It also provides an explanation of other expressions commonly found in documents relating to pension schemes.

Accrual Rate — The fraction of earnings for each year of service which forms the basis of entitlement under a final salary scheme, commonly $\frac{1}{60}$ or $\frac{1}{80}$ for each year of pensionable service.

Accrued Rights — The benefits of service up to a specific date frequently calculated in relation to current earnings or projected final earnings.

Additional Voluntary Contributions (AVCs) — Where additional benefits upon retirement may be secured under an employer's scheme by a member paying contributions over and above his normal contributions (if any). Total contributions to the scheme, including AVCs, must not exceed 15 per cent of gross earnings.

Approved Scheme — A retirement benefits scheme, including a personal pension scheme, approved by the Inland Revenue.

Buy-out Plans — The purchase by pension scheme trustees of an insurance policy (with or without dependants' rights) to replace the benefits which a member is entitled to under the pension scheme and which are given up by the member when he leaves the scheme.

Commutation — The exchange of pension benefits for a tax-free single lump sum payment.

COMP — Contracted-out money purchase scheme.

Continuation Option — Where a member leaves a pension scheme which provided life assurance benefits and the insurance company underwriting those benefits offers the member the opportunity of continuing his cover under the life assurance policy. The option must normally be exercised within a limited period after leaving the scheme.

Contracting Out	The ability to contract out of the State earnings-related pension scheme (SERPS), which forms part of the State pension. If an occupational pension scheme is contracted out, the scheme must provide members with a guaranteed minimum pension. Contributions to the State scheme in respect of employees who have contracted out are reduced.
Convertible Term Assurance	Where, during the existence of the policy, the insured may convert the policy to either whole life assurance or endowment assurance, without the need to produce further medical evidence of health.
Death-in-service Benefit	Benefits available on death of employee before retirement. Typically a lump sum payment or return of contributions.
Decreasing-term Assurance	A variant of the basic term assurance policy, by which the amount of cover is reduced each year.
Defined Contribution Scheme	An alternative term for a money purchase scheme (q.v.).
Earnings Cap	The maximum amount of earnings that may be pensioned which will attract income tax relief. Applies only to certain categories of individual. The current earnings limit for an occupational pension scheme or paid to a personal pension scheme is £75,000 (1992/93). The earnings cap applies to all schemes established after 14 March 1989. It does not apply where members of a scheme established before that date joined before 1 June 1989.
Endowment Assurance	A policy effected for a specified term with a lump sum payable at the end of the term or upon the prior death of the insured. Premiums are payable throughout the term.
Executive Pension Plan	Pension arrangements made available to selected directors or employees.
Exempt Approved Scheme	A scheme approved by the Inland Revenue enjoying taxation privileges specified by statute. Approval will generally require the scheme to have been established under an irrevocable trust.

Final Salary Scheme — An occupational pension scheme where the benefits are calculated by reference to the member's pensionable earnings at or near the time of retirement or upon leaving service. The benefits are usually $\frac{1}{60}$ or $\frac{1}{80}$ of the pensionable earnings for each year of pensionable service.

Free-standing AVCs — Where a member of an occupational scheme may make an additional contribution to another scheme which is completely separate. The total of the member's contributions to both schemes must not exceed 15 per cent of his remuneration.

Funding — The overall amount which the employer/employee is required to pay to achieve the relevant pension benefits. In final salary schemes, the funding rate, expressed as a percentage of pensionable earnings, is determined by the scheme actuary and remains in force for the period until the actuary next reviews the scheme, which currently takes place every three years.

Guaranteed Minimum Pension — The pension (or part of pension) payable to a member of a contracted-out scheme; it is normally equal to that part of the State pension which is given up by virtue of the contracting-out arrangement.

Hancock Annuity — A type of immediate annuity purchased by an employer when an employee retires.

Insured Scheme — A scheme where contributions are paid to an insurance company which undertakes, in return, to pay some or all of the benefits provided under the scheme.

Integration — A pension which is designed to take into account part or all of the State scheme benefits.

LAUTRO — Life Assurance and Unit Trust Regulatory Organisation.

Linked Qualifying Service	Actual service under an earlier pension scheme (whether with the same or a different employer) which results in a transfer credit under a subsequent scheme (because a transfer payment is made from one to the other) and which is, therefore, taken into account for preservation purposes.
Lower Earnings Limit	The minimum amount which must be earned before National Insurance contributions become payable. The current lower earnings limit (1992/93) is £54 per week. Once the limit is exceeded, contributions are payable in respect of earnings both above and below the limit. A member of a contracted-out scheme will pay reduced National Insurance Contributions.
Managed Fund	An actual fund as opposed to an insurance company's general pension business fund. Units of a managed fund are referable to particular pension schemes. The investment of the fund is managed by an insurance company.
Married Woman's Property Act Policy	A policy which is written in trust under the Married Woman's Property Act 1882, s 11, for a stipulated class of beneficiaries.
Money Purchase Scheme	A scheme where benefits are determined by the level of contributions paid and the performance of investments, as opposed to a scheme which provides benefits related to earnings. On retirement, an annuity is purchased for the member.
Nomination	Where a member indicates to the trustees his wishes as to the destination of the death benefits under the scheme. The trustees are not, however, bound by a nomination.
OPB	Occupational Pensions Board.

Occupational Pensions Scheme — A scheme established by an employer to provide pension benefits for employees and their dependants upon the employee's retirement or death whilst in service. Contributions must be made by employers and may be made by employees, depending upon the terms of the scheme.

PSO — Pension Schemes Office, formerly known as the Superannuation Funds Office (SFO).

Pensionable Earnings — The earnings on which benefits and/or contributions are calculated. Pensionable earnings may differ from actual remuneration in that they may exclude various items such as bonuses, overtime and commission.

Pensionable Service — Employment which qualifies as years of service, by reference to which a member's benefit entitlement under a pension scheme is normally calculated.

Personal Pension Scheme — A scheme made available by a commercial provider (whether insurance company, building society, bank or unit trust group) for one or more unconnected individuals who contribute to the scheme. Final pension depends on the level of contributions made by the individual and the performance of investments in the fund or funds. These schemes are designed to replace retirement annuity contracts but are aimed at both employees and the self-employed.

Preservation — Where a person who has been a member of a scheme for at least two years cannot forfeit benefits under the scheme by leaving it.

Protected Rights — That part of a personal pension scheme or contracted-out money purchase scheme that represents the fund accumulated by contributions paid by the DSS. These rights are separated from any other benefits built up by the member's or employer's contributions.

Relevant Benefits — A term defined for the purposes of taxation. It comprises any benefits connected with retirement or death, except for benefits given only in the event of accident.

Retirement Annuity Contract — A contract between an individual and an insurance company for the provision of benefits on retirement or upon death. The fund produced by the contributions is managed by the insurance company. After 1 July 1988, these can no longer be taken out – personal pension schemes having been introduced as a replacement. The amount of pension payable under existing contracts depends on the level of contributions made and the performance of investments. These contracts are also known as section 226 policies.

Section 226 Policies — Retirement annuity contracts.

Self-administered Scheme — A scheme where the assets are invested by trustees or through an external investment manager.

SERPS — The State earnings-related pension scheme forming part of the State pension. The scheme adds an earnings-related component to the basic flat rate pension based upon contributions on earnings between the lower and upper earnings limits.

Simplified Scheme — Simplified schemes may be set up on a money-purchase basis or on a final salary basis. They have been designed in order to speed up the process by which pension schemes are approved by the Inland Revenue. If the benefits under the scheme are exactly as set out in specimen documents produced by the Pension Schemes Office and membership excludes controlling directors, approval of a simplified scheme will be given automatically.

Small Self-administered Scheme — Schemes for directors who have a 20 per cent or greater interest in their company and who are therefore precluded from being a member of the company's occupational pension scheme.

State Pension — Payable from national insurance contributions made by employees and employers. Provision is in the form of a flat-rate pension and a State earnings-related pension (SERPS) which, taken together, aim to provide an individual with a pension equal to one-half of his average earnings.

Statutory Scheme A retirement benefit scheme set up by statute or statutory instrument for public sector employees and approved for the purpose by a minister or Government department.

SFO Superannuation Funds Office, now renamed the Pension Schemes Office (PSO).

Term Assurance A policy having only a specified duration and providing for a lump sum to be payable if the insured dies within the specified period. Premiums are payable throughout the term.

Top Hat Scheme An alternative term for the executive pension plan.

Transfer Payment A payment made by the trustees of one pension scheme to the trustees of another. Such a payment is normally made when a member leaves one employment to take up another and wishes to join the pension scheme available by virtue of his new employment. The payment enables the receiving pension scheme to give additional benefits which will reflect the contributions made to the paying scheme. Such payments may also be made from occupational pension schemes to personal pension schemes where an employee or former employee elects to join such a scheme.

Unapproved Scheme Allowed by virtue of the Finance Act 1989. Benefits can exceed those of approved schemes but some or all of the tax relief of approved schemes is unavailable.

Unit-linked Pension Scheme A scheme where the amount of retirement benefits is related to the units in an investment fund and the value of the fund varies according to the value of the units.

Upper Earnings Limit The maximum limit on which National Insurance contributions are payable (approximately seven times the lower earnings limit and currently £405 per week (1992/93)).

Vested Rights The benefits under a scheme to which a member would be unconditionally entitled if he were to leave the scheme. These rights may include related benefits for dependants.

Whole-life Assurance A policy effected for the whole of the insured's life with a lump sum payable only on death. Premiums are usually payable until death or until the insured reaches a specified age.

APPENDIX

Precedents

1 Questionnaire pursuant to Family Proceedings Rules 1991, r 2.63 – life policies

2 Questionnaire pursuant to Family Proceedings Rules 1991, r 2.63 – pensions

3 Consent order – life policy
 (a) Undertaking to take out life policy
 (b) Undertaking to authorise insurers to release information
 (c) Undertaking to undergo medical examination
 (d) Undertaking to assign life policy
 (e) Order transferring life policy

4 Consent order – pension

5 Order for lump sum by instalments

6 Deferred lump sum order

7 Letter to insurance company requesting policy details

8 Form of authority

9 Letter to employer/trustees requesting information relating to a pension scheme

10 Expression of wishes/nomination form

11 Deed of assignment of a life policy

12 State retirement pension forecast: Form BR19

13 Letter of instruction to actuary to value occupational pension rights

14 Tracing request: Form PR4

Precedent 1 QUESTIONNAIRE PURSUANT TO FAMILY PROCEEDINGS RULES 1991, r 2.63 – LIFE POLICIES

Please provide the following information in respect of every life policy on [Petitioner's/Respondent's] life and/or of which he is a beneficiary, either actual or potential:

1 (a) the insurance company;
  (b) policy number;
  (c) type of policy;
  (d) the sum assured;
  (e) premiums payable;
  (f) maturity date.

2 An up-to-date quotation from the insurance company showing the surrender value including bonuses (where applicable).

3 An up-to-date quotation from the insurance company showing the projected sum inclusive of bonuses payable on maturity (where applicable).

Precedent 2 QUESTIONNAIRE PURSUANT TO FAMILY PROCEEDINGS RULES 1991, r 2.63 – PENSIONS

Please provide the following information relating to the [Petitioner's/Respondent's] Pension Scheme/any Pension Scheme of which the [Petitioner/Respondent] is a member.

(1) A copy of the Trust Deed, the Rules of the Scheme, any explanatory booklet available to its members and the last Annual Report of the Trustees together with details of any material change.

(2) The [Petitioner's/Respondent's] date of joining the scheme.

(3) Are there any transfers in from another scheme?

(4) Has the [Petitioner/Respondent] agreed any special terms with his employers not contained in the information supplied in response to (1) above?

(5) What is the [Petitioner's/Respondent's] anticipated normal retirement age?

(6) The [Petitioner's/Respondent's] latest benefits statement not more than 12 months old.

(7) A statement from the Trustees of the Scheme (or some other appropriate source) explaining and quantifying the projected benefits on retirement both on the basis that contributions continue at the present rate until retirement and on the basis that no further contributions are made, such information to include:

 (a) the lump sum payable in the event of the [Petitioner's/Respondent's] death in service;
 (b) the spouse's/dependant's pension payable in the event of the [Petitioner's/Respondent's] death in service;
 (c) the maximum lump sum which the [Petitioner/Respondent] could receive in part commutation of his pension on retirement;
 (d) the pension in the event of such commutation;
 (e) the pension which the [Petitioner/Respondent] will receive upon retirement on the basis that he does not elect to commute part of his pension for a lump sum;
 (f) the spouse's/dependant's pension payable in the event of the [Petitioner's/Respondent's] death after retirement.

(8) A statement of the current transfer value of the [Petitioner's/Respondent's] pension fund if [he/she] were to leave service.

 (g) Please give details of any material condition from which the [Petitioner/Respondent] is suffering which might materially affect the [Respondent's/Petitioner's] rights under the scheme.

Precedent 3 CONSENT ORDER – LIFE POLICY

(a) *Undertaking to take out life policy*

AND UPON the [Petitioner/Respondent] undertaking to the court that [he/she] will within [ ] days from the date of this order take out with [ ]/[a reputable UK] insurance company a policy of assurance on [his/her] life [for a term of [ ] years]/[for the whole of [his]/[her] life]/[to mature on [ ]] in the sum of £[ ] [[With/Without] profits] for the benefit of the [Respondent/Petitioner/child of the family], the [Petitioner/Respondent] further undertaking to the court promptly to pay all premiums due in respect of the said policy and to do nothing which might prejudice or invalidate the said policy until the [Respondent's/Petitioner's] death or remarriage whichever shall be the earlier; the Petitioner and the Respondent agreeing that all benefits under the said policy, whensoever arising, shall be paid to the [Respondent/Petitioner] or [his/her] estate and that the [Petitioner/Respondent] shall have no beneficial interest in the policy or its proceeds at any time.

Note: It may be appropriate to amend the form of undertaking to enable the benefit of the policy to revert to the husband in the event of the wife's prior death or remarriage. Similarly, where a policy has a surrender value, provision must be made for what is to happen to the policy monies if a child predeceases the life assured – are the proceeds to fall into the child's estate or go to the life assured?

(b) *Undertaking to authorise insurers to release information*

AND UPON the [Petitioner/Respondent] undertaking to the court irrevocably to authorise [ ] insurance company to release to the [Respondent/Petitioner] such information as [he/she] may from time to time require relating to policy numbered [ ].

(c) *Undertaking to undergo medical examination*

AND UPON the [Petitioner/Respondent] undertaking to undergo such medical examination as may be required by an insurance company to enable the [Respondent/Petitioner] to insure [his/her] life.

(d) *Undertaking to assign life policy*

AND UPON the [Petitioner/Respondent] undertaking to the court to assign within [ ] days from the date of this order to the [Respondent/Petitioner] [his/her] [interest in] the life assurance policy numbered [ ] effected with [ ] insurance company; [the Petitioner/Respondent] further undertaking to the court to pay all premiums as and when they fall due in respect of the said policy until such time as the [Respondent/Petitioner] shall remarry or die [*or as appropriate*].

Notes

1 Notice of assignment must be given to the insurers.
2 This particular undertaking provides for an absolute assignment whereby the policy proceeds will go to the assignee irrespective of whether he/she remarries or predeceases the life assured.
3 This undertaking could and should be dealt with by way of an order (see (e)). However, an undertaking will be appropriate if the parties wish to record and implement the agreement reached prior to decree absolute.

(e) *Order transferring life policy*

UPON the [Petitioner/Respondent] undertaking to the court to continue to pay promptly the premiums on the life policy effected by the [Petitioner/Respondent] with [ ] insurance company policy number [ ] ('the life policy') until the [Respondent's/Petitioner's] death or earlier remarriage.

IT IS ORDERED that:

[1] The [Petitioner/Respondent] shall transfer to the [Respondent/Petitioner] within [ ] days of the date of this order [his/her] [interest in] the life policy.

Precedent 4 CONSENT ORDER – PENSION

UPON the [Petitioner/Respondent] undertaking to the court that he will forthwith irrevocably nominate the [Respondent/Petitioner/child of the family] to receive [ ] per cent of the lump sum payable in the event of his death in service under his pension scheme with [ ] insurance company or such other scheme of which he may from time to time be a member and to provide written evidence of receipt of the nomination form from the trustees of the scheme upon request by the [Respondent/Petitioner].

Precedent 5 ORDER FOR LUMP SUM BY INSTALMENTS

The [Petitioner/Respondent] do pay or cause to be paid to the [Respondent/Petitioner] a lump sum of £[ ] payable by instalments as follows:

(a) As to £[ ] within [ ] days of final decree herein [*or as appropriate*];
(b) As to the further sum of £[ ] on or before [ ] 19[ ];
(c) As to the balance on or before [ ] 19[ ].

[AND IT IS DIRECTED that if the [Petitioner/Respondent] fails to pay any instalment to the [Respondent/Petitioner] on the due date the whole of the lump sum of £[ ] shall become payable forthwith to the [Respondent/Petitioner]]

[AND IT IS [FURTHER] DIRECTED that interest shall be payable by the [Petitioner/Respondent] at the rate applicable for the time being to a High Court judgment debt on the said instalments from [ ] 19[ ] [*date no earlier than the date of the order*] until the dates on which the said instalments are respectively due to be paid.

Notes:

1 The court has jurisdiction to order interest until the date when the instalments fall due for payment under MCA 1973, s 23(6). Thereafter, interest will be payable automatically under the County Courts (Interest on Judgment Debts) Order 1991 (SI 1991/1184) on a lump sum order made by a divorce county court for £5000 or more after 1 July 1991. Similarly, interest runs automatically from the date due for payment on any High Court lump sum order under the Judgments Act 1838.
2 Where the balance payable under (c) is expressed as a flexible sum (eg calculated as a percentage of the lump sum payable to the husband on retirement), see precedent 6.

Precedent 6 DEFERRED LUMP SUM ORDER

[Upon the [Petitioner/Respondent] undertaking to the court to continue contributions of £[ ] per [month/year] to the [ ] Scheme until the [Petitioner's/Respondent's] retirement on [ ] save and except for the [Petitioner/Respondent] being obliged to accept early retirement on the grounds of redundancy, invalidity or ill-health]
BY CONSENT IT IS ORDERED that:
[1] The [Petitioner/Respondent] do pay or cause to be paid to the [Respondent/Petitioner] a lump sum [of £[ ] payable within [ ] [days/weeks/months/years] of the date of final decree herein [*or as appropriate*]]/[equal to [ ]% of the lump sum payable to the [Petitioner/Respondent] upon his retirement under the [ ] Scheme on condition that the [Respondent/Petitioner] shall not have remarried at the date of the [Petitioner's/Respondent's] retirement]
AND IT IS DIRECTED that interest shall be paid by the [Petitioner/Respondent] at the rate applicable to a High Court judgment debt from [ ] 19[ ] [*date no earlier than date of the order*] until [ ] 19[ ] [*date when lump sum is due to be paid*]

Notes:

1 MCA 1973, s 23(6) enables the court to order interest 'until the date when payment of the [lump sum] is due'. Thereafter, interest will be payable automatically under the County Courts (Interest on Judgment Debts) Order 1991 (SI No 1184) on a lump sum order made by a divorce county court for £5000 or more after 1 July 1991. Similarly, interest runs automatically from the date due for payment on any High Court lump sum order under the Judgments Act 1838.
2 Provision may be necessary to cover the possibility of the husband dying before payment of the deferred lump sum.
3 See generally **6.4.1.3**.

Precedent 7 LETTER TO INSURANCE COMPANY REQUESTING POLICY DETAILS

Our Ref:

Dear Sirs

Life Assured:
Policy Number:

We act for [ ] of [ ]. We enclose our client's signed authority to yourselves to provide us with information in respect of the above policy.
We should therefore be obliged if you could let us have the following details:

(a) type of policy;
(b) the sum assured;
(c) the beneficiaries under the policy;
(d) premiums payable;
(e) maturity date;
(f) an up-to-date quotation showing the surrender value (if applicable) including reversionary bonuses to date;
(g) an up-to-date quotation showing the projected sum (if applicable) inclusive of reversionary and terminal bonuses (where applicable) payable on maturity.

Please quote our reference above when replying.

Yours faithfully

Precedent 8 FORM OF AUTHORITY

To: [*Name and address of insurance company*]

Life Assured:
Policy Number:

I, [ ] of [ ] hereby authorise you to provide my solicitors, XYZ & Co, of [ ] (Ref:) with details of the above policy.

....
Signature

Dated this [ ] day of [ ] 19[ ]

Precedent 9 LETTER TO EMPLOYER/TRUSTEES REQUESTING INFORMATION RELATING TO PENSION SCHEME

Dear Sirs

Member:

We act for [ ] of [ ]. We should be obliged if you could provide the following information in relation to his pension.

1 A copy of the Trust Deed, the Rules of the Scheme, any explanatory booklet available to its members and the last Annual Report of the Trustees together with details of any material change.

2 Please indicate when our client joined the scheme.

3 Has our client transferred into your scheme any rights under another scheme?

4 Are there any special terms relating to our client which are not dealt with in the information provided under 1 above?

5 A copy of our client's latest benefits statement.

6 A statement explaining and quantifying the projected benefits on retirement, both on the basis that contributions continue at the present rate until retirement, and on the basis that no further contributions are paid, including:
   - (a) the lump sum payable in the event of our client's death in service;
   - (b) the spouse's/dependant's pension payable in the event of our client's death in service;
   - (c) the maximum lump sum which our client could receive in part commutation of his pension on retirement;
   - (e) the pension in the event of such commutation;
   - (e) the pension which our client will receive upon retirement on the basis that he does not elect to commute part of his pension for a lump sum;
   - (f) the spouse's/dependant's pension payable in the event of our client's death after retirement;
   - (g) please indicate the normal retirement date on which the projections requested above have been based.

7 A statement showing the current transfer value of the Pension Fund if our client were to leave service.

Yours faithfully

Note: The letter will, of course, require amendment to reflect the information which the client has already been able to provide.

Precedent 10 EXPRESSION OF WISHES/NOMINATION FORM

To the Trustees of the [ ] Pension Scheme

Date:

Dear Sirs

I write to give you details of the arrangements which I would wish you to put into effect in the event of my death prior to the death of my wife ('W').

1 In the event of my death prior to a decree absolute of divorce from W all death benefits to be paid to her.

2 In the event of my death after decree absolute of divorce from W:

(a) if neither W nor I have remarried, all death benefits to be paid to her;
(b) if W has remarried and I have not remarried, all death benefits to be paid to her;
(c) if W has not remarried and I have remarried, any lump sum payment arising from my death to be paid to W and the widow's pension to be paid to my widow. In the event of no such lump sum being payable, the widow's pension to be divided equally between W and my widow [*or as appropriate*];
(d) if both W and I have remarried, all death benefits to be paid to my widow.

I understand that this is only an expression of my wishes, which is not binding upon the trustees.

Yours faithfully

Note: The nomination form should be sent to the Trustees/Employer together with a copy of the court order.

Precedent 11 DEED OF ASSIGNMENT OF A LIFE POLICY

THIS DEED OF ASSIGNMENT is made the [ ] day of [ ] 19[ ] BETWEEN [ ] of [ ] [(hereinafter called 'the First Assignor')] [and [ ] of [ ] (hereinafter together called 'the Assignors)] of the one part and [the said] [ ] of [ ] (hereinafter called 'the Assignee') of the other part

WHEREAS:

(1) A policy of assurance was issued by the [ ] Insurance Company on the [life]/[joint lives] of the Assignor[s] dated [ ] 19[ ] and numbered [ ] the sum of £[ ] [with/without profits] was assured to be paid [on [ ] 19[ ]/20[ ]] [[or] on the [earlier] death of the [first to die of the] Assignor[s]/[on the death of the Assignor before [ ] 19[ ]].

[(2) By a Deed of Assignment dated [ ] 19[ ] the said policy of assurance was assigned by the [First Assignor]/[Assignors] to the [ ] [Building Society]/[Bank PLC]].

[(2)/(3)] On [ ] 19[ ] an order was made by District Judge [ ] in the [ ] County Court in proceedings between the [Assignors]/[the First Assignor and the Assignee] bearing number [ ] whereby inter alia the [First] Assignor [was ordered]/[undertook] to transfer to the Assignee all [his/her] interest in the said policy of assurance [and the Assignee undertook to pay all sums payable thenceforth under the said policy of assurance].

NOW THIS DEED WITNESSETH as follows:

1 The Assignor[s] as [trustee[s]]/[beneficial owner[s]] HEREBY ASSIGN[S] to the Assignee all the interest of the Assignor[s] in or under the said policy of assurance and all monies assured by or to become payable under or by virtue thereof and all benefits and advantages thereof TO HOLD the same unto the Assignee absolutely subject to the payment of all future premiums on the said policy [and subject to the charge dated [ ] 19[ ] in favour of [ ] [Building Society]/[Bank PLC].

2 The [First] Assignor covenants with the Assignee:

2.1 Not to vitiate policy

[The]/[Every] policy assigned above is now valid and in full force and that the [First] Assignor will not do omit or knowingly suffer anything by which [the]/[any such] policy may become void or voidable or the Assignee or anyone claiming title through [him]/[her] be prevented from receiving the money assured by the polic[y]/[ies] or any bonus or addition to [it]/[them];

2.2 To do things necessary to keep policy on foot
That if by reason of anything done omitted or knowingly suffered by the [First] Assignor [the]/[any such] policy shall at any time become voidable the [First] Assignor will immediately at [his]/[her] own cost take all such action as shall be necessary for keeping the policy on foot and in particular if any payments over and above the yearly premium of £[ ] shall become payable in order to keep on foot the policy the [First] Assignor will punctually make all such additional payments and will indemnify the Assignee and all persons claiming title through [him]/[her] against all such payments PROVIDED ALWAYS that nothing in this sub-clause shall impose on the [First] Assignor any liability to pay the yearly premium of £[ ];

2.3 To effect and assign new policy
If by reason of anything done omitted or knowingly suffered by the [First] Assignor [the]/[any such] policy shall at any time become void the [First] Assignor at [his]/[her] own cost will immediately effect with an insurance company approved by the Assignee or other person entitled immediately before that time to the void policy a new policy for such sum as would have been payable under the void policy if the Assignor[s] [or one of them] had died immediately before that policy became void and will execute an assignment of the new policy to the assignee or other person so entitled and will pay any sums payable by way of premium under the new policy over and above the annual sum of £[ ] and will keep the Assignee and all persons claiming through [him]/[her] indemnified against all such excess sums.

[2]/[3] The Assignee covenants with the [First] Assignor that [he]/[she] will henceforth punctually pay the said monthly premiums for keeping the said policy on foot and that [he]/[she] will keep the [First] Assignor and [his/[her] personal representatives effectually indemnified against all actions proceedings costs claims and demands whatsoever in respect thereof.

[3]/[4] The [First] Assignor and the Assignee HEREBY DECLARE[S] that notwithstanding the foregoing provisions of this Deed the expressions 'the yearly premium of £[ ]' and 'the annual premium of £[ ]' shall mean the premium of £[ ] and any increase in the premium from the commencement date of the policy payable due to any alteration of the law AND HEREBY AGREE that the [First] Assignor shall not in any event be liable to pay such an increase in the premium from the commencement date of the policy payable due to any alteration of the law AND HEREBY AGREE that the [First] Assignor shall not in any event be liable to pay such an increase in the premium.

[4]/[5] We hereby certify that this instrument falls within category H of the Schedule to the Stamp Duty (Exempt Instruments) Regulations 1987.

IN WITNESS whereof the parties hereto have hereunto set their respective hands the day and year first before written

SIGNED AS A DEED by the said
[ ] in the presence
of:

SIGNED AS A DEED by the said
[ ] in the presence
of:

Precedent 12 STATE RETIREMENT PENSION FORECAST: FORM BR19

SOCIAL SECURITY

How you can get a Retirement Pension Forecast

You can get a Pension Forecast if you are –

- a woman under 59 years 8 months
- a man under 64 years 8 months

All you have to do is fill in the attached form and send it to us at –

Department of Social Security
RPFA Unit
Room 37D
Newcastle upon Tyne
NE98 1YX

If you want more information about Retirement Pension generally, ring Freeline Social Security – a free and confidential service. Just ring 0800 666 555.

What your Pension Forecast will show

Basic Pension

This is the part of your State Retirement Pension that depends on the National Insurance you pay in the time you would normally be working.

Your forecast will tell you ▶

- the amount of Basic Pension in today's money that you can expect to get based on the National Insurance you have already paid.
- the amount of Basic Pension in today's money that you can expect to get based on the National Insurance you have already paid and any future National Insurance you are likely to pay.
- what, if anything, you can do to get a better Basic Pension.

Additional Pension and contracted-out deductions

Additional Pension is the part of your pension that depends on your earnings since April 1978.

A contracted-out deduction is paid by your employer's contracted-out occupational pension scheme. It is the least amount of occupational pension that you must be paid and you get instead of all, or part of, your Additional Pension.

Your forecast will tell you, in today's money ▶

- the amount of Additional Pension, taking account of any contracted-out deduction, that you can expect to get based on the National Insurance you have already paid.
- the amount of Additional Pension, taking account of any contracted-out deduction, you can expect to get if your earnings go up at the same rate as inflation.
- the amount of Additional Pension, taking account of any contracted-out deduction, you can expect to get if your earnings go up at 1.5% more than the rate of inflation.

Graduated Retirement Benefit

This is based on the amount of graduated National Insurance you have paid.

Your forecast will tell you ▶

- how many units of Graduated Retirement you have and what they are worth in today's money.

If you are widowed or divorced

Your late or former spouse's National Insurance can sometimes be used to help you get a better pension.

Your forecast will tell you ▶

- the amount of pension, including Basic Pension, Additional Pension, Contracted-out deduction, and Graduated Retirement Benefit, that you can expect to get using your late or former spouse's National Insurance.

BR19

Printed in the U.K. for H.M.S.O. 3/91 Dd 8357733 C2700 38806 G3807

SOCIAL SECURITY

Request for a Retirement Pension Forecast

Personal details

Please give us the following details –

National Insurance (NI) number

Title Mr/Mrs/Miss/Ms

Surname

Other names

Other surnames you have had
This may have been your name before marriage

Date of birth / /

Address

Postcode

Daytime phone number

1 Living abroad

Have you ever lived outside England, Scotland and Wales since you were 16?

No ☐

Yes ☐ Where did you live?

Please turn over ►

2 Marital status

We need to know what your marital status is. This is because your Retirement Pension may be affected by a spouse's National Insurance (NI) contributions.
We use spouse to mean your wife or your husband. Please tick the description that applies to you, and answer the questions.

Single	☐	*Go to Question 4*		
Married	☐	What is your date of marriage?	/ /	*Go to Question 4*
Married but about to get divorced	☐	What is the expected date of the divorce?	/ /	*Go to Question 3*
Divorced	☐	What was the date of the divorce?	/ /	*Go to Question 3*
Widowed only tick this box if you are a woman	☐	What date were you widowed on?	/ /	

Are you getting any Widowed Mother's Allowance or Widow's Pension?

No ☐ *Go to Question 3*

Yes ☐ What is your reference number?
This is on the front of your order book or on the letter that we sent to you about getting your benefit paid direct into an account. ______

---

3 We need more information if you are
- **married but about to get divorced, or**
- **divorced, or**
- **widowed.**

Please tell us about your marriage.
If you have been married more than once, only tell us about your last spouse here.

The date of your marriage / /

Your spouse's full name ______

Your spouse's date of birth / /

Your spouse's National Insurance (NI) number ☐☐ ☐☐ ☐☐ ☐☐ ☐

Your spouse's last address
If this is different to the address you have written at the beginning of this form.
______
______
Postcode

---

4 Were you widowed before April 1978?

You only need to answer this question if you are a woman.

No ☐ *Go to Question 5*

Yes ☐ Have you remarried since April 1978?

No ☐

Yes ☐ What date did you marry your late husband? / /

What date were you widowed? / /

What date did you remarry? / /

5 About what you are doing now

We need to know what you are doing now.
Please tick any of these descriptions that apply to you.

Working for an employer ☐

Self employed ☐

Not working ☐

Signing on as unemployed ☐

6 About National Insurance

We need to know what National Insurance contributions you are paying at the moment.
Please tick the description that applies to you.

Paying full rate NI contributions ☐

Paying reduced rate NI contributions ☐

Paying voluntary NI contributions ☐

Not paying any NI contributions ☐

7 About Benefits

We need to know if you are getting any of the benefits listed here.
Please tick any that you are getting.

Dependant's War Pension ☐
(this is sometimes called War Widow's Pension)

Industrial Death Benefit ☐

Statutory Sick Pay (SSP) ☐

Invalidity Benefit ☐

Severe Disablement Allowance ☐

Invalid Care Allowance ☐

Job Release Allowance ☐

Unemployment Benefit ☐

Child Benefit ☐

What is the date of birth of your youngest child or only child? [/ /]

What is the date of birth of your oldest child if you have more than one? [/ /]

If you get your Child Benefit paid by order book, is your name above the main address on the cover of the book? No ☐ Yes ☐

If you get your Child Benefit paid into a bank or building society account, is your own name and address shown on the letter about Child Benefit we send you once a year? No ☐ Yes ☐

8 Extra information

Your Pension Forecast will tell you

- how much Retirement Pension you are already entitled to
- how much Retirement Pension you will be entitled to when you are
  60 (for a woman)
  or 65 (for a man)

if you pay NI contributions until then.

We can also tell you what may happen to your Retirement Pension in different situations. If you want extra information in your forecast, please tick the things you want to know about.

Working after age 60 (woman) or 65 (man) ☐ Please tell us the date you may go on working till. [/ /]

Stopping work before age 60 (woman) or 65 (man) ☐ Please tell us the date you may stop working. [/ /]

Going abroad ☐ Please tell us the country that you might go to. [ ]

Paying full rate NI contributions after having paid reduced rate NI contributions ☐ Please tell us the date you might change. [/ /]

Please tell us what your annual earnings are now. [£]

Change of marital status ☐ Please tell us what you think your marital status might change to.

Married ☐ on [/ /]

Divorced ☐ on [/ /]

Widowed ☐

Paying NI contributions that have not been paid in the past ☐

Change in annual earnings ☐ Please tell us what they might change to, or the % that they might go up. [ ]

Your signature

Now please sign and date this form.

Your signature [ ]

Date [/ /]

What to do now

Check that you have answered all the questions that apply to you.

Send the form to us at –

Department of Social Security
RPFA Unit
Room 37D
Central Office
Newcastle upon Tyne
NE98 1YX

Precedent 13 LETTER OF INSTRUCTION TO ACTUARY TO VALUE OCCUPATIONAL PENSION RIGHTS

Our Ref:

Dear Sirs

We act for Mrs [ ] of [ ] in divorce proceedings. Her husband is a member of the [ ] pension scheme and we would be grateful for your opinion as to the value of the following losses suffered by our client under the scheme upon decree absolute of divorce:

(a) loss of widow's pension;
(b) member's benefits;
(c) death benefits.

In order to assist you, we enclose:

(a) [a copy of the trust deed, the rules of the scheme and] an explanatory booklet relating to the scheme; [*Note 1*]
[(b) replies received from our client's husband's solicitors providing information relating to the scheme [in response to a questionnaire served on behalf of our client, an extract from which we also enclose]]; [*Note 2*]
[(c)].

The background information which you will require is as follows:

1 Date of marriage: [ ]

2 Full name of wife: [ ]

3 Date of birth: [ ]

4 Full name of husband: [ ]

5 Date of birth: [ ]

[6 [Names of children and dates of birth]]

7 The husband's salary is £[ ]. [However, the husband's pensionable salary is £[ ] [*include source of information*]]. The definition of the husband's final salary is to be found [ ]

8 [Husband's date of commencement of employment and date of joining pension scheme (if different)]

[9 Any special (unfunded) terms such as a promise of two-thirds pension irrespective of service]

[10 No benefits have been transferred into the scheme from another scheme relating to any previous employment [*or as appropriate*]]

11 [Information regarding the health of the parties]

Please let us know if you require any further information and let us have an estimate of your charges before undertaking your valuation.

Yours faithfully

Notes: 1 The explanatory booklet will usually suffice if up to date

2 See precedent 2

Precedent 14 TRACING REQUEST: FORM PR4

APPENDIX 4

Registrar of Pension Schemes

Tracing Request

PR4

To search for a pension scheme in the register of occupational and personal pension schemes

About you

1 **Your name**

2 **Your address**

Postcode

What you should do

If your enquiry is about a pension scheme run by a former employer, fill in the section headed "About the employer", below, or

If your enquiry is about a personal pension scheme, fill in the section headed "About the personal pension scheme", over the page.

Lastly, please read **15** , **16** and **17** on page 3.

About the employer

Please write the last known name and address of the employer whose pension scheme you are enquiring about

3 **Employer's last known name**

4 **Employer's trading name (if different to 3 above)**

5 **Employer's last known address**

Please also give any other name and address under which the employer has been known

6 **Employer's previous name**

7 **Employer's previous address**

If you were employed at an operating unit within a large organisation and you know who the employing company or corporation was, please give its name and address

8 **Name of employing company**

9 **Address of employing company**

IF YOU WISH TO ENQUIRE ABOUT A SECOND SCHEME, YOU MUST FILL IN A SECOND TRACING REQUEST FORM

Please turn over

About the personal pension scheme

10 Scheme's last known name

11 Address at which the management of the scheme was conducted

12 Please give any other name under which the scheme has been known

13 Please give any other address at which the management of the scheme was conducted

Any additional information

14 Please give any other details that you think may help in tracing the pension scheme (eg type of work, when you worked there, head office address of employer if there was more than one address, scheme name if your scheme was an occupational pension scheme).

What to do now

15 **Please make sure the form is filled in, then sign it below.**

16 **Please send the form to the address shown at the bottom of the page.**

17 Declaration:

(a) I declare that I am the person who is, or may be, or may become entitled to benefits under the scheme which I am trying to trace, or

(b) I am a person or representative of a body acting on behalf of such a person.

The name of the body is:-

Please delete (a) or (b) as appropriate.

Your signature	
Name (Please use capitals)	
Date	

18 **If you are representing an individual and wish the reply to this application to be sent to you, please give your address.**

Send this form to

Registrar of Pension Schemes
Occupational Pensions Board
PO Box 1NN, Newcastle upon Tyne NE99 1NN
Tel: 091-22-56393/4

INDEX

References in the index to roman numerals are to the Introduction.
References to paragraph numbers are to the main text or Glossary.
References to Appendix numbers are to the precedents within the Appendix.